Birds against Men

Louis J. Halle, Jr.

BIRDS

AGAINST

MEN

Drawings by Lynd Ward

New York · The Viking Press · Mcmxxxviii

Preface

No book, immediately recognizable as such, should need a preface. I take it that a book is something complete in itself, the vehicle of its author's comment on the world as he knows it, and that additional comment outside the body of the book is likely to be, in some sort, a confession of weakness. The author, fearing that his readers will find him out anyway, betrays himself in advance.

Where the unity of a book is not immediately apparent, however, another purpose may be served by appending a comment. If it is a collection of essays, for example, there is some point to revealing the circumstances under which they were collected, so that the reader may be guided in his approach to them. This book hardly comes under that designation, though at first glance it might appear to. It does not bring together scattered pieces written at different periods. These chapters, revealing one person's experience of the ways of birds and men, were all written in the course of one year, or a little more, during which he devoted himself to that task and no other. They represent one continuous effort. Each chapter was written for the book alone, and with a view to its place in the whole. Each was written because it was necessary to complete the picture. So much for the mechanics.

When it comes to speaking of the intimate aspects of the book that constitute its true unity I am more hesitant.

Though sometimes written in a frivolous manner, it was nevertheless written with a serious, even a pretentious, purpose. That pretension is cause enough for hesitation. A writer is judged by what he attempts and must guard himself against attempting too much. He must bite off no more than he can chew. Having taken the original bite over a year ago, however, I can no longer hope to escape its consequences. Possibly I could not have attempted less in any case. To convey something of my enthusiasm for bird-life would have been a sufficient goal. But to do that I had to reveal something of the basis for that enthusiasm, which was no isolated frenzy, and that meant bringing all sorts of things into the picture. I had the choice of painting a stuffed bird lying with its feet in the air on a laboratory table, or painting it on the wing in a setting that included the world. Not being a laboratory man, I cannot see that I had any real choice. I had to take a pretty big bite out of the world in order to get my bird. The pretension, though not immediately apparent, was part and parcel of the original purpose. It forced me to refer to mankind, a subject I would never have dared to deal with directly. Not that I have used the world of birds as a blind for observations on our human world. Even if I had dared to tackle the subject directly I would sooner or later have found it necessary to bring birds into the picture, and the result might have been much the same.

Why, particularly, birds? The question is unanswerable, unless I say merely because I know more about bird-life than I do about the life of plants, mammals, insects, or other forms of nature. It would have been my bias, had I written on the subject of men, to have regarded them and their works as an integral part of the scheme of nature which the birds, it so happens, represent to my mind. Someone else with the same bias and a special interest in, say, mammals, might have written such a book and left the birds out altogether. One must allow something to caprice.

Apart from the way in which they were written, then, there is an internal unity that makes these chapters a book. Ostensibly a collection of separate experiences of birds, they present one experience and one world.

Contents

ARRIVAL FROM THE SOUTH

Arrival from the South

MY encounter with the being whom I call Lucy occurred about the beginning of March. I offered
her the name as a sort of makeshift to cover the
nakedness of her anonymity; but without success, for she
persists in my memory to this day as a mysterious and name-
less daughter of the wild. My intention was chivalrous: to
give her a new start in life, an identity of her own within
the security of our human world, after her own world had
rejected her as unfit for survival. But she refused the name
and all it meant, preferring her proper doom to an improper dependence on strangers. Looking back on the brief
and fruitless hours of our acquaintance, I feel like one of
those peasant hosts of legend who unwittingly received into
their poor abodes gods in disguise or saints in sackcloth.
But her identity, though it was intimated to me, was never
revealed. She came in humbleness and in humbleness she
departed, against my wishes, after one short night.

That winter the weather, according to our local authori-
ties, had been the coldest known in these parts in living
memory. Every year the meteorologists of our village, which
lies just beyond grasp of New York City, assemble about
the counter of Schelling's general store to exchange their
findings and come to the same conclusion. Every year the
local thermometers explore new depths. The weekly news-
paper, published a few miles away but with a department

devoted exclusively to our doings, recorded seventeen degrees below zero (Fahrenheit) that year; but the enthusiastic local boys did better. Twenty degrees was first offered across the counter; someone else offered twenty-three; and before the meeting broke up it had been decided that this was the coldest winter on record, with an all-time low of twenty-eight degrees below zero. Everyone was exhilarated by the thought.

Another dictum of the local wise men was that it would be a phenomenally late spring. Witness the winter, which had not begun to make itself felt in any extraordinary degree till almost the middle of February. Already in the first week of March, we had just had the bitterest weather of all: the familiar landscape of fields and shrubs, and stone walls that run over the hilltops and down through the valleys, had disappeared under a prodigious visitation of snow that came down overnight and smothered every landmark of our usual world. The cold spell came right on top of the snow. For two days a heavy north wind blew and the sky was a brilliant sheet of frost matching the landscape below it. Not a cloud ventured over the horizon into its frigid expanse; the thermometer dropped steadily. The sun shone like a glittering star, cold and comfortless; and, what with the fresh snow, you could hardly open your eyes at all out of doors.

It was then that Lucy appeared, in the guise of a hooded merganser, a little brown duck, fan-crested and without a name. I found her one morning at the upper end of Trinity Lake, where it curves about like the bent-over top of a pear and comes to a point at the juncture of the stem that feeds it. A crippled wing had kept her behind when the freeze came and her mates escaped to open southern waters, and she had remained to starve with her wing quills frozen to the ice. Despite her terror, equaled only by her helplessness, I dug her out and brought her home, where she sailed around in the bathtub for the rest of the day. She carried herself jauntily, like a toy duck in a department store, her cinnamon crest raised in a fan, her head back on her shoulders, her narrow, toothed bill pointed straight before her— and occasionally she gave a short bewildered bark, like a sea-lion's, that was totally unexpected in such a delicate creature. But she was in a nightmare world far away from home. She dove and raced about at the bottom of the bathtub like a terror-stricken fish every time I came into the room, and refused to take notice of the offerings I made her from a tin of sardines (the very best) bought at Schelling's for the purpose. Her wild merganser spirit, accustomed to running brooks and swampy woodlands where man is at best a trespasser, could not fathom this neat tepid world of porcelain fixtures in which she suddenly found herself. Within its narrow confines food was unthinkable, a fish no longer a fish, to be gulped and eaten. For nothing in this new life had her previous experience or the inherited wisdom of merganser generations prepared her. No wildest dreams of merganser madness could have conceived such a thing.

I wish I could say that my patience as a host, my tireless efforts to make her feel at home, to obtain her acceptance of my hospitality as the lesser of alternative evils, eventually reconciled her to a tame life among human friends. Her only chance of survival, since she was already under sentence of death in her own world, was to forgo her past and take on a new identity under the shelter of this sanctuary that was offered to her in a new setting. But she was indissolubly wedded to the wild. The laws that governed her being were the stringent laws of nature, not the merciful laws of man, and if those laws decreed doom it was her humble destiny to submit. She could not accept the asylum I offered. She could not take a human name.

Having failed in my blandishments, I went down the next morning (while the thermometer stood at sixteen below), a pickax over my shoulder and a doomed duck under my arm, to cut a swimming-hole for her in the pond near the house. I knew then that my mission was funereal, that in reality I was preparing a watery grave. The naked duck did not feel the cold—it was her element—but it struck the man, bundled up as he was in layers of heavy clothing, with a muffler about his face, a cap over his ears, stout boots and woolen mittens to protect his extremities, like the breath of a hostile world, ready to punish his invasion with petrifaction. A grave silence, the silence of a world in which no living thing moves, pervaded the landscape, interrupted momentarily by the painful crackling of frozen trees and the soft whistle of the north wind through their branches. Outside the house it was a merganser world, hostile to man, who adventured into it at his peril. In deathly silence it waited to reclaim its own.

I set the duck down on the ice and for an hour swung the pickax against the frozen surface, retreating occasionally to the house, my face hoary with icicles, to recover a little warmth. Soon the heavy slabs I had cut were floating about on the surface of a steaming gap in which the water showed like an expanse of polished obsidian. Little clouds of vapor rolled away over its surface. When I was done, I picked the merganser up and launched her from the edge of the ice-pack without ceremony. No sooner had she touched the water than she dove, dipping her head and disappearing as though a thread attached to her bill had jerked her down from below. I saw her swim away into the cavernous depths beneath the ice, to return a minute later, bob up to the surface like a celluloid duck in a goldfish bowl, catch a breath of the cold air, and vanish below again. But the gap would not stay open. The second time she returned the crystals that spread rapidly out from its border had left only a little opening in the center. She swam about under the transparent surface like a fish, wings close to her sides, neck extended, crest flattened against her head, before she finally found the hole and bounced out. In another few minutes she was sitting in a pool of water exactly the size and shape of her body. The wound in the ice had healed up hard against her.

I did my best for her, but it was hopeless. No one could cope with that malevolence. I piled the heavy chunks of ice up on the edge of the pool and cut more; I widened the hole as fast as I could, slashing at the film that formed as I worked. But time was on the other side. Winter undid my work after me, sealed up the hole behind my back, and in the afternoon the anonymous body to which I had vainly offered a name was stretched out flat on the unbroken surface of the frozen pond. Nature was accomplishing the merganser's destiny despite my efforts to rescue her from it. Already the little flame of her life had flickered so low that it had finally become imperceptible.

The glittering sun sank colorlessly against the snow-bound ridges to the west and winter prevailed, like an invisible phantom, allowing no life, no movement, and no hope to show itself out of doors. The few birds and beasts that had remained to suffer under it, owls and bluejays and squirrels, huddled in the dense evergreens and were silent. All night the north wind whistled around the corners of the house, besieging the land with a cold fury, and in the morning the stiff body of the merganser was lying frozen in a drift of snow.

That it would be a late spring there could be no doubt. Beneath that sky hope lay, like the little duck, frozen in the snow. In the whole cloudless expanse there was no grain of comfort, no token of a merciful dispensation for a benumbed world that awaited in silence the advent of a new season. Under its spell one relinquished belief in a fate that keeps the seasons moving in their appointed rounds and allows none to hold sway indefinitely.

But hope is immortal. The morning after the merganser was put to death I awoke late to hear a steady dripping from the eaves of the house. The north wind, as if the sacrifice of the duck had fulfilled its purpose, had given way to a soft breeze from the south. The landscape had darkened under the sky. A stream of warm air washed gently over the hilltops, brushed the stark limbs of the trees, and rustled the dried stalks of grass that the north wind had exposed. The stillness was emphasized by the monotonous dripping. Wherever you went you could hear the dull sound, as of fingers moving under the snow. The sun, which for days had looked down on the land like the eye of conscience in a puritan soul, became warm and friendly, a beneficent power that sided with the coming dispensation. A new buoyancy was in the air, a feeling of impending cosmic changes, as though one heard the machinery of that great clock preparing to strike.

The new season gave warning of its imminence in the

muffled claps of thunder that reverberated below the frozen surface of Trinity Lake. Trinity Lake is completely enclosed by steep slopes wooded with hemlocks, massive and ancient. It lies just across the road, a stretch of water about three-quarters of a mile in length and at some places not more than a stone's throw wide. Its name comes from the three original pools that, when the dam was built at the near end, merged their separate identities in a perfect union. Even now you can see where the pools must once have been by observing how the two shorelines approach and recede from each other. The heavy woods and abrupt slope of its banks make hard going in summer, and the possibility of meeting poachers makes trespassing in that season something less that a peaceful procedure. I can remember two distinct occasions when I almost had my head blown off for my pains in driving the pirates away. One Irishman was whistling in a small flock of scaup when I happened along, just as they were coming within range of his gun. I made a dash for the water's edge, picked up the first stone handy, and hurled it at the ducks, which took off down the lake as one and came back high overhead on their way to other feeding grounds where they might again hope to be undisturbed. But the Irishman had already spent three tense hours of that morning seducing them with his calls, and did not relish having success snatched from the muzzle of his gun as he was about to press the trigger. He made some rather loud and threatening noises, but stopped short of violence when he saw that I was equally indignant. Again, I had a big Italian from the city point his shotgun at my head. He and a companion had been shooting grouse when I came along and, without any authority at all, ordered them off the place. I brazened the matter out till, after a few moments, he lowered his gun and marched off peacefully. But those few moments, which seemed to spin themselves into eternity, left me strangely limp. I prefer the lake in winter, when I can walk over its frozen surface instead of wrestling with bushes that obstruct the narrow path along its edge, and when I can have it all to myself; or, if I must share it, have to contend with only a few fishermen who drop their lines through holes in the ice. For fishermen follow a peaceable pursuit, and we get along together.

Judged by its appearance on this early March morning the lake might have been solid ice from its smooth surface to its rugged depths, like an inverted iceberg that fitted perfectly into every irregularity of the hollow between the wooded slopes. But there was something more, something articulate, down there. Momentarily a dull explosion would break from below, an abrupt release of sound that rocketed across the lake like billiard balls over the taut skin of an immense drum, ending against the muffled shores almost as soon as it had begun. Beneath the surface that was so utterly lifeless something new and portentous stirred. One of those periodic changes of nature was just commencing; life moved in the womb, and at intervals the lake shook with the agony.

In the woods along shore the winter birds, more subtly attuned than man to the transformation of the seasons, more keenly aware of impending changes in the cosmic sphere, had suddenly begun rehearsing their spring songs. The bluejays gave the riot-call, blew their shrill police-whistles urgently, warning all predatory hawks and owls that order would be maintained, if only by their own disorderly activity. They shrieked ORDER, ORDER, ORDER, blew their whistles hysterically; the blue-coated riot-squads dashed back and forth through the trees, trying to locate some object for their activity, a sleeping owl or a peaceful hawk. The crows came out like the black-watch vigilantes at the call of the police, streaming over the treetops toward the scene of violence, cawing raucously. They massed on the tall evergreens with a hoarse clamor, as much as to say that the situation, however desperate, was not beyond their control. Let the red wing of anarchy but show itself in those ancestral woods and they would give it something to remember! But the cowardly disturber, whoever he was, refused to come into the open, the wing of anarchy was not to be seen. The bluejays, as if satisfied at the disturbance they had created, returned quietly to their ordinary daily pursuits, and after a few minutes the crows, tired of a sport that had no object, a pursuit without a quarry, left the scene to resume their interrupted feeding in the marshes.

Now that reasonable quiet had been restored I could hear the chickadees once more. They moved through the dripping woods in little bands, bouncing about among the twigs like so many jumping-beans, chattering incessantly as if to urge one another on to the unending search for particles of food hidden behind flakes of bark. Occasionally one would take a short respite, prompted by this new buoyancy in the air that seemed worthy of at least a moment's introspection, mount to the top of a tree, and, with a sudden plaintiveness that voiced all the immense melancholy of noble spirits held in bondage to the stringent and unremitting requirements of nature, sing his two soft and piercing chickadee notes, uttering the descending scale of his sorrow with a depth of feeling whose existence could hardly have been suspected in a mere feathered automaton. He made you feel what a vale of sorrow this world is, after all, full of creatures designed, like Samson Agonistes, for greatness and nobility, and caught in the sordid treadmill of mortal existence. "O glorious strength, put to the labour of a beast, debased lower than bond-slave!" Having uttered his mild plaint, the little chickadee would drop down again to renew his hurried inspection of bark and twig, the cultivation of his garden, chattering merrily once more as if he had entirely forgotten what a tragic figure he really was.

In the afternoon I went up over the hill where the skeletonesque steel windmill stands, its fan, responsive to the changing winds of the four seasons, pointing south now and revolving gently, and on down the path that leads through the woods to the Meadows. In these Meadows the mysteries of nature have their innermost sanctum. If any change is contemplated in the universe by the powers that hold sway over it, I feel sure it will first manifest itself in this long expanse of swamp that seems so placid and inviting, so quiet and pastoral, but defies you to penetrate its marshy reaches. In winter there is treachery beneath the snow. You put your foot down anywhere with unpredictable results. It may land on a hummock that will support it, or it may land on a stretch of ice that will give way under your weight and let you down into a bottomless bog. Long lines of brittle alders wind through the marsh, indicating the river-beds (we call almost anything a river in this region), the areas of deep water, but enticing you like the will-o'-the-wisp to follow them into still denser jungle and deeper water. When you bog down through the ice suddenly, waist-deep in the cold stream, you grasp at their

branches in vain. They bend willingly to your weight or
come away completely in your hand. At the lower end
the alders become thick and impenetrable over a wide area.
But I have never yet learned to arm myself against their
seduction, the temptation to invade their fastness for the
mystery within, though the reward is always the same: an
icy bath, mud-filled boots, an assortment of cuts and bruises.
It is precisely because you cannot get at the heart of the
Meadows that their profundities seem so portentous. Time
and again I have followed the flowing water deep into the
wilderness, wading to my waist and bending close to the
surface to keep clear of the overarching branches and
thorn-bushes. I have gone in there with an ax, cutting a
long, circuitous path through a forest of dead and dying
trees that rise above the alders. But no matter how deep
you go, the mystery always scuttles away from the path
ahead of you, and when you arrive, there is only silence.
In winter a rabbit may stand motionless on the ice and
await your approach, or a pheasant may burst with a sudden clatter from the near-by bushes and sail off over the
treetops, but these are nothing compared to the countless
sounds that you hear and can make nothing of.

The Meadows were a scene of desolation when I came
out from the edge of the woods. In the woods the snow was
a heavy blanket that obliterated all the ground-marks. Its
edges had already begun to recede from the tree-trunks, and
everywhere it was punctured by holes from the intermi-
nable dripping. It offered a sullen resistance to my passage,
and the cavities left by my rubber boots quickly filled with
water. But in the Meadows the thaw was further advanced.
The long expanse of dead hummocks and broken cattails
was still buried in an irregular blanket of snow through

which the dry stalks showed, but everywhere water was flowing under the surface. You could hear the rustling murmur of its passage, and now and then a bridge of snow between hummocks would suddenly collapse. Out in the center, as I could see from the higher land on the other side (I had taken the muddy path across the upper end of the Meadows), there was already an extensive area of open water.

It was not a heartening sight. The sharpness of winter, the severity of its emptiness, the authority of its silence, like an ultimatum written in the sky, may be cruel, but it is clean; it commands your respect. The thaw is welcome only for what it portends. Its task is negative and menial, undoing winter in anticipation of another season. There is nothing cheering in this sullied freshness, this dissolution of the landscape. Stripped of its glamour, the earth has the disquieting appearance of a house that is being cleaned out after one boarder in preparation for a new one, its rooms bare, its furniture in disarray, its floors damp and noisome.

My usual path runs through a grove of trees on the far side of the Meadows toward the lower end. That patch of woods looks particularly miserable in winter. The trees, growing in sandy soil, have a stunted and dead appearance; their limbs are rotten and break at a touch. They had nothing to offer today, no promise to make. They merely dripped, sullenly, as if that were part of their character, a life-long habit. But from the lower end of the Meadows, where the cluster of dead trees stands in the center of the alder jungle, a hairy woodpecker was drumming furiously on a dry limb. Occasionally he would utter his loud bleat and dart away in a long undulation to the next tree, where he would resume his drumming, as though he were tele-

graphing some indecipherable but vital message to a dripping world that paid no attention. This was about as much
as one could expect from nature after the ravages of winter: a few crows and bluejays, an occasional company of
chickadees, a woodpecker. It would hardly have been worth
walking out to see these, had it not been for the unreasonable stirring of hope.

At the lower end of the Meadows the path leads up a little hill from which you can look directly over the jungle of
alder in the hollow below. The top of this hill is the best
standpoint I know for attending the change of seasons.
The alder bushes, the dead trees, the hemlock forest that
occupies the tall knoll beyond, and the long sweep of open
marsh are all spread out before you. There are no houses
and no men to disturb the ordinary course of nature. The
birds that come through on their migrations find good
refuge here, shelter to suit varying tastes in the dense
swamp grass, the alders, or the hemlocks. The ducks find
running water or stagnant, as they please. Food is abundant: bugs and berries for little birds, game for hawks.
During the migrations there are few inland birds known
to this part of the world that may not be found in this
short segment of the landscape that you can take in at a
glance. It is outfitted to receive and offer hospitality to all
visitors.

I waited a long while in the cold on top of that snowy
hill, as though I were keeping an appointment with someone less punctual, and I scanned the southern horizon
anxiously, filled with a strange and potent hope against
which I armed myself vainly with the expectation of disappointment. To be kept waiting at a tryst to which you
have long been looking forward is a peculiarly harrowing

experience. Such occasions can be almost intolerable with suspense. The same suppressed and anxious emotion took hold of me that afternoon on the appointed hilltop. I knew from our Gregorian calendar, an astronomical table worked out to a fine degree of accuracy by generations of scholars using the infallible rules of mathematics, that the sun was well on its way to the equinox, that the spheres had already given the cue to nature. I had heard the muffled whir of wheels in the great cosmic clock which rules the destiny of men and birds, and I waited tensely now for the first sound of its striking.

The migratory passage of birds, like the movements of the stars, can be a great consolation to men whose minds continually search for an established order and progression in the universe. The knowledge that, whatever we may make of ourselves in the moment of our existence, the stars will continue in their appointed courses, the seasons will move in their confirmed order, the birds will pursue their destined biannual migrations, carries with it a sense of ultimate security which the works of man alone fail to convey. It seems to give us the intimation of a will that directs us, it belies our orphaned estate in the universe. Order, harmony, regularity, those elements implicit in the recurrent flight of birds, are beyond the touch of the good and evil that men do in the numbered hours of their survival. Knowledge of the integrated pattern of the universe in which the birds share, of the final cosmic autocracy whose imposed limits no organism may transcend, secures us from the nightmare of anarchy.

But the consolation we derive from knowledge of fate is not enough. We are not like the stars, dead clods in space with no will of our own. We cannot tolerate the degradation of tyranny. Within the limitations that give meaning to our existence we must have room for the exercise of our own volition, however pitiful it may appear before the universal will. For without that liberty living beings cease to live, men become cogs in a machine. The stars symbolize the tyranny of a brazen machine-universe; they are fixed in their orbits by inflexible rules, their movements are minutely predictable. But the flight of birds is, within its limits, capricious. The migrations, though they take place year after year, are never predictable. They are never twice the same. In the endless and conflicting variety of living individuals whose wills are sovereign within the confines of nature, the birds confirm free men in the exercise of their freedom. In that mirror of nature we recognize ourselves as independent individuals who can accept the order of the universe or combat it; in either case, though weakness make us helpless, asserting our dignity as free individuals by naming our choice. The flight of birds epitomizes a dual world of tyranny and liberty, of order and whimsy, of fear and of hope, within which everything is possible for mankind from the highest heroism to the most abject degradation. Who would cavil, then, at being kept waiting for the inevitable? If punctuality is the courtesy of kings, only death, the greatest sovereign of them all, is invariably punctual.

It was evident that this year spring was going to be late. Except for the drumming woodpecker and an occasional bluejay crying, the Meadows were utterly barren, silent and desolate. They waited beneath an empty sky that gave no sign of ever changing; they waited dumbly for the inevitable—for the uncertain. When I had been standing attentive in the snow for a long hour, the empty

boarding-house at last began to have its effect on my confidence. After all, I told myself, reasoning against a wholly unreasonable disappointment, little could be expected so soon
after such a severe spell of winter. It was still too cold, and
the prospect too dismal. Tomorrow, maybe, or the next day.
. . . Having come to a decision, I swallowed the hope that
had possessed me all day, and was about to turn away when
my eye was arrested. . . .

To the south, where the horizon dips in a V between hills,
in that little triangle of sky, my attention was caught by
something so dim that it might have been merely an aber-
ration of vision. But it was enough to halt me in my tracks
and hold me there till it became distinct. Despite the firmness of my expectations, the urgency of my hopes, I stared
now at the first faint token of their fulfillment with in-
credulity. In that gray gap, monotonously matching the
snow-bound hillsides that flanked it, I could make out a
little company of black motes growing rapidly larger. The
birds of the company formed a compact phalanx, all bobbing up and down in the mass like so many balls in the
hands of an adroit juggler. As they drew closer I could
distinguish the sable uniforms, the rounded wings, the
strange softness of flight as though the air through which
they flew were some denser substance. Along that channel
that led up from the south, from the permanent home of
the hot seasons, life was again moving forward before the
annual impulse of spring. The sky might still have been
loaded with unfallen snow, veiled and opaque, like a
gray web stretched between the hills. But the new boarder
had sent word of her approach. The flight of birds, established since earliest times as an omen of cosmic purpose,

made manifest the inscrutable will, foretold the movement of the unknown, revealed the invisible.

There was something in the progress of this advance-guard as it approached that told of countless legions to the rear. This was not a capricious maneuver of the cohorts, a detached visitation, but the spearhead of a universal advance on all fronts, sure of itself and as deliberate as fate. Over the far distances of two hemispheres, over the jungles and white-capped seas, over hills and valleys and plains, along the winding course of great rivers, across bleak stretches of desert, between clouded mountains and through deep gorges, from one ocean to another and beyond, the hordes were already sweeping. They came from the frigid wastes of the Antarctic; they came from the jungle of the Amazon; they came from the islands of the sea. Some, such as the flocks of geese and ducks in flying-wedge formation, swept across the skies beyond my horizon with the impetus of a cavalry charge. Some, like the swallows and the hawks, followed a more leisurely course, foraging the country as they went. Others moved up only by the nocturnal light of the stars. But all swept on without hesitation and without thought, sure of their strength and firm in their purpose, with the crushing momentum of the inrushing tides of the sea. These dancing motes came like the spray of an advancing wave, they were the first cohorts of a mass movement unequaled in its grandeur by any other manifestation of life on this earth.

As they arrived overhead, all the birds whirled and dropped together, like leaves in a cat's-paw of wind, landing in the topmost branches of one of the trees that rose above the alders and becoming instantly motionless. The tree at once appeared to be covered with knobs. I glanced at my watch and made a mental note of the time, then raised my glasses to study the new arrivals.

The birds were obviously exhausted from a long migration. They remained fixed to the branches, motionless and silent; like the inanimate birds of a colored engraving, their forms and markings could be studied at leisure. And all were the same, bright black, even to the eyeball and legs and the sharp bill, with only that jaunty military slash across the wing, the insignia of the male red-winged blackbird, to relieve their sinister appearance. As I waited, another uniformed squadron moved up through the channel from the south and settled over the branches of another tree in the swamp; and then one squadron after another, coming at regular intervals in parade formation, in that invincible progress of masses on the march, till all the trees that rose up above the alders were knobbed with the silent forms of the companies at rest. The whole aspect of the Meadows had been changed: they reposed quietly, their silence continued undisturbed, but the waiting was over and the peace that rewards suspense seemed to lie upon their frigid surface, to become part of their silent and enduring passivity. . . .

Suddenly, as though all had been simultaneously touched by the same vagrant impulse, as by a gust of wind, the birds of the first squadron dropped from their perches, floated down into the alder bushes on set wings, and were immediately lost to sight. But now that they had rested and were intent on feeding, they found their voices. A flurry of cluckings broke out in the alders, like stones rolled together, occasionally interrupted by a shrill whistle—and then, momentarily, the long, triumphant conquering peal,

the strident bugle-call of the male, the wire-drawn cry of
his pride and lustiness that begins with an abrupt call to
attention and hangs on in the air. The other companies
followed as soon as they too had rested, and in a moment
the Meadows were totally different. They were no longer
desolate, as they had been all winter, for now the sound of
the blackbirds filled them from end to end, evoking all the
throbbing life, the passion, and the abundance of a spring
that had been half forgotten.

A late writer, discussing what he called the Ethics of
Elfland, commented on the renewed wonder with which
an elfin spirit meets every dawn. He finds a fresh surprise
and gratification each time the sun rises, knowing that in
terms of his ethics the fact that the sun always has risen
puts it under no compulsion to go on following its own
precedent. There is enough of the elf in all of us to feel
that same sense of magic, that awe of the occult powers, at
the totally unnecessary confirmation of the expectations
they arouse in us. To stand waiting for spring to come, on
a certain hill, at a certain moment, on a day that gives no
sign of impending arrival, and then actually to have it
come, making its entrance with the dramatic suddenness
of a heroine who knows how to calculate her effect!—what
is that if not the highest cosmic magic? Really (I can tell
the truth now), I had not quite credited my own belief
that there was a changeless order in nature, a time and tide
to which its affairs were subject. It was so easy to suppose
it merely a wishful illusion, prompted by the hope of a
paternity and the fear of chaos. The confirmation of my
stubborn faith, like the touch of a magic wand, dispelled
the clouds of doubt, renewed my strength worn thin over

the long winter, restored my confidence in a purposeful world, in an unfailing sunrise obeying the dictates of the immutable government to which we are all bound.

Doubtless the wise men gathered about the counter in Schelling's store, huddled in heavy overcoats and caps to protect them from the chill of winter, were still shaking their heads over the prospect of a late spring, and wondering whether it would ever come at all. The grayness of the sky and the bleak monotony of snow-covered hills betrayed no new presence to their vision. They heard no revealing voices. But I had witnessed the flight of birds, and had they asked me I could have told them, like one who cried in the wilderness, that the dawn of a new and better day was at hand.

BY SOVEREIGNTY OF NATURE

By Sovereignty of Nature

IF some observer had been perched on one of those lovely
white clouds that sailed overhead, following my irregular movements about the edge of the Meadows and
through the various patches of woodland, he might have
thought I was merely an aimless nature-lover straying afield
of a June morning to enjoy the splendor of the first summer's day. Of course, the burlap sack which hung limp on
my back might have given him pause. It was enough to
make any observer suspicious. An empty sack over a man's
shoulder has definite connotations; it smacks of the nefar-
ious. Yet the serenity of the scene alone would have quieted
suspicion.

And the day was undoubtedly beautiful. It seemed as if
suddenly, this morning, the spring foliage had reached its
summer fullness. It drooped motionless from the trees of
its own weight, blanketing the woods with heavy green
masses. Insects droned in the sunshine, approaching and
receding; little clouds of gnats suspended in the air shim-
mered as though they were penetrated by invisible heat
waves; yellow butterflies drifted across the open Meadows
to brush the luxuriant fringes of the woods with their
wings.

But this morning I had no eyes for the splendor of nature.
I was, definitely, a man with a purpose. Taking my bear-
ings by an oak that stood out above the other trees, I skirted

the woods till I had found the overgrown wagon-tracks I
was looking for. They entered the woods at right angles and
immediately plunged into darkness, where they continued
a dim existence along the edge of a morass. The sunlight
broke against the leaves above and fell in fragments. An
invisible ovenbird periodically cracked the cathedral stillness with an abrupt crescendo of song. But my attention
was elsewhere. When I found a certain landmark I turned
from the trail; a hundred paces more across marshy hummocks brought me to the brink of a stream that wandered
through the shadowy swamp. This was my goal. Above me,
high in the crotch of a silver birch, was a massive platform
of dead branches, with two fledgling hawks peering intently
down at me over its edge.

It all goes back to a bleak day at the end of March. In
my notes for that day I recorded seeing "a pair of red-
shouldered hawks in woods of S. W. Meadows engaged in
domestic activities conducive to the fertilization of eggs."
That brief statement, of course, hardly tells the story: it
is entirely too dispassionate to evoke, for anyone but me,
the fierce passion of the actual courtship. I could not, in
the pages of a loose-leaf book devoted only to the briefest
factual notations, have allowed myself to observe that the
mating of those wild hawks was a natural phenomenon
comparable to an earthquake or a storm at sea. Only the
date and place were necessary for the record.

March 27 and woods of S. W. Meadows. I had, so to
speak, a grandstand seat for the performance, on that little
hill at the south end of the Meadows that overlooks the
surrounding woods—the hill from which I had observed
the arrival of the first red-winged blackbirds a few weeks
earlier. It was still the candid season, before the earth had

buried itself beneath the summer luxuriance of grass and foliage. From that hilltop one's vision traveled far through the tangle of stark limbs in the woods below. The two big birds were so absorbed in their courtship that my presence went unnoticed. They charged back and forth through the maze of branches in a series of dashing maneuvers, turning abruptly to avoid collisions, intermittently repeating in series the wild, explosive, two-syllabled cry of their kind. Having proved his skill at obstacle flying, the male suddenly left the female for a display of power flight, rising on beating wings in a steep spiral from the treetops. The unreasoned intention was, undoubtedly, to impress her with his strength and lustiness, his fitness to be the father of her hawklets. But she took the performance for granted. Sweeping low through the woods, she braced her pinions and rose to the naked limb of a dead chestnut that stood out above the surrounding trees, where, with shaking wings, she attended the fateful moment of his descent.

The male was so high now that I had momentarily lost him; but the unbroken series of screams still invaded every corner of the landscape. Silent and receptive, the earth seemed, like the female, to be waiting with suspended breath for the thrill of the plunge. This moment was entirely his. While it lasted he was the repository of all passion, of all hope, of all adventure, the resplendent guardian of the seeds of creation. Suddenly his screams broke off; wings collapsed against body as he turned over and began to fall back towards the patch of woodland where the female waited. Far below, the earth seemed to have stopped revolving. An intense silence had come over it. The speck grew like a storm-cloud in process of formation, accelerating as it approached until, low over the woods, wings were

partially spread and its course leveled off. Like a streak of
rust through the gray and lifeless woods the male hawk
shot below the treetops in the direction of the quivering
female. As he swung up screaming behind her, the female
crouched low, letting her wings hang loose—and at the
climactic moment Akbar was conceived. In the white heat
of that union all his nobility, the unequivocal jealousy of
his dignity and the fierceness of his pride, had its catastro-
phic inception.

I have good reason to believe that this was the occasion.
The mating performance was repeated before me only
once more, almost a week later, and of the two hawks that
were brought into being that season Akbar was the senior
by almost a week.

There are several ways in which one might approach
Akbar's character, and literary precedent vouches for them
all. Characters have been described, as Dickens described
them, with emphasis on the aberrant. They have been described with emphasis on their humanity, as in Shakespeare.
They have been described heroically, in the folk-sagas of
primitive peoples, as the naked embodiments of basic
ideals. The Dickensian method is out as far as Akbar is
concerned. I doubt that he was an odd character, and in any
case I have no standard of normality to go by. I might adapt
the Shakespearean technique to show his essential hawkishness torn by the hereditary conflicts of his hawkish psy-
chology. But in the immense simplicity of his being there
were no such conflicts; his hawkishness was always integrated and serene. What is left, then, except to describe
him as the embodiment of that basic ideal of hawkishness
which underlies and transcends all its particular mani-

festations? Akbar, like Siegfried, could never be set in a novel or drama. His proportions are definitely epic.

It may be objected that I have no right to indulge in any sort of fiction in these pages. Legend may do well enough in its place, but this is, after all, a sober factual record of birds and of events that once had a concrete existence. The bones of Akbar, scattered somewhere beneath the humus, would still testify to that, as do his parents, who still return each spring to rear their brood in our vicinity. Siegfried, because he represented an ideal conception of man, was never a man at all, but an immortal god. Of Akbar's mortality there can be no doubt; one cannot escape the vision of those bones. Yet (and here I betray for the first time the essence of his character) Akbar, by virtue of the immense simplicity of his kind, was at once hawk and hawk-god, at once an individual and an ideal. When you are dealing with the primitive you cannot disassociate the two. Only the complex creatures that civilization produces are capable of such division. Men, for example, manage to survive despite the fact that few approach the physical ideal of the Hermes of Praxiteles, just as the fat and flabby dog manages to exist by means of the civilized amenities of hearth and table while his brother the wolf, unless he is strong and lean and alert, cannot exist at all. It takes no Praxiteles, apprehending ideal proportions from the depths of his imagination, to depict the ideal hawk, for each individual hawk illustrates in himself the perfection of his kind. Far from indulging in legend, I am strictly realistic when I regard Akbar as an epic hero, a Siegfried in the world of hawks.

In appearance he was the perfect expression of sheer Hawk, the peer of any bronze eagle that ever guarded a gateway or mantled his wings over the tomb of a fallen soldier. Even when I first retrieved him from the wild in that piece of sacking and brought him to the empty garage that was to be his lifelong home, before his natal down was more than half covered by the new plumage, he was a terrible masterpiece of undiluted hawkness. There were really two hawks in the middle of that cement floor: the adult, represented in the incomplete plumage—the short tail that was still well above the ground, the white breast feathers with brown streaks along the shafts, the mottled brown of wings and back, the vaguely striped and furry feathering of the head—and the nestling whose white down showed through his uniform like the cotton stuffing in a torn mattress. Ignorant of his character, you might have been tempted to laugh at his motley. What might have made him especially ludicrous in your eyes was a topknot of feathers which rose to a point on his head. But you would not have laughed long, for you must almost instantly have become aware of those two dark eyes under beetling brows that had in their fixed stare no reciprocal pleasantness, but the fierce challenge of their wildness. You would as soon have laughed at the infant Hercules' blue ribbons after you had seen him strangle the serpents with his naked hands. One of the guileless human beings who had observed his arrival, deceived by that topknot into thinking that his advances might be met in the friendly spirit in which they were offered, smilingly stretched out his hand to within a foot of Akbar's head and immediately withdrew it with a gasp. So quickly that the eye could not follow the movement, Akbar had struck with one of his talons and torn a gash right across the palm of the man's hand. No one even smiled after that.

Though I took extraordinary pains with Akbar from the start, I never succeeded in reducing his wildness; he never became what you could call a tame bird; and that despite the fact that he soon flew willingly enough to my hand when I whistled and allowed me to stroke the soft and heavy plumage which had, in a surprisingly short time, reached its full growth. But he was always just making the best of circumstances. He never came to my hand because it was my will, but only because it was his wish. And the first chance he found to return to the wild and independent life for which he was born he left me. The tragedy that attended his recapture put an end forever to that independence.

The first few days were the hardest. In one corner of the garage Akbar occupied a bed of straw on top of a large wooden box and took his raw meat from the sharpened end of a stick, which I held in my hand, by striking with one talon, transfixing it with his sickle claws as though it had been a live mouse that might dart away from him if he relaxed his grip. But, being a true hawk, he never began to feed on his prize without allowing at least a minute to elapse after its capture. In the hawk world it is not proper form to begin devouring one's prey until there has been time for its quivering to stop. Hunger, no matter how imperative, must wait on this questionable mercy. Whether it has been an osprey with a fish or a sparrow hawk with a lizard, I have never yet seen a hawk fail to carry out this formality. Akbar would stand in attendance on his piece of meat, clutching it with the grip of death, his feathers ruffled up and his wings mantled to hide it from me (as I supposed), his eyes fiery with challenge, till the time required by convention had elapsed. Then he would reach down, hook his sharp upper mandible in one corner of the flesh, and pull upward against the pressure of his feet to tear away a morsel small enough to swallow; and such a morsel might be anything up to the size of an overgrown mouse. When those mandibles were parted wide, the gullet presented the appearance of a good-sized mouse-hole, the thin blade of a tongue forked at the back to retain the booty. And he never used his beak except in tearing food apart, not even in drinking, for he abstained wholly from liquids. When I offered him a piece of flesh, he invariably took it with a swipe of his foot, and I used to impress incredulous visitors by dangling his meat several inches above his head, where it was just out of reach of his beak, so that they might watch him bring it down with one unerring stroke of his claws, like a cat.

It may be noted that all these were traits of the wild hawk and entirely unnecessary to Akbar in his captivity. They illustrate what I mean by saying that he never showed any signs of becoming domesticated. He never exchanged his hawkhood for the ignoble status of a pet dependent on others for his livelihood, like the dog on the hearth, with his fat sides and blunted teeth. A more adaptable creature would soon have found out for himself that it was not necessary to allow a moment of grace before eating meat that was already as dead as it would ever be. But Akbar, like the inflexible aristocrat he was, clung to the immemorial traditions of his caste even when the change of circumstances had robbed them of their original meaning. He remained unreconciled to his environment, he refused to give up the ceremonial ways of his noble lineage for a mess of human pottage.

It was because of this uncompromising affirmation of his

identity that one could not treat Akbar with the affectionate contempt accorded to pets, those pseudo-children who
are educated to their humble station by a process that
nullifies their birthright, revokes the selfhood of their
species. He never surrendered one jot of that birthright.
We confronted each other, hawk to man, independent and
equal creations of nature in the fullness of our integrity.
He learned no human ways, and I never attempted to teach
him any. I had no desire to see his hawkhood degraded to
the level of the dog who walks on his hind legs, and such
a desire would in any case have been powerless to prevail
against its inflexibility. I still recall painfully the spasm of
horror with which I came to my senses after I had cuffed
him in a stroke of rage prompted by a wound he had given
me when I attempted too great a familiarity. I felt like a
peasant who had struck an emperor, and for a few anguished minutes I could see no other course than to cut
off my hand in atonement. The incident was never repeated, though I have cuffed dogs since with no other feeling than one of righteousness. Dogs belong to my world,
but I had no authority over the hawk.

During those weeks in which Akbar was being inducted
into human society the history of man might have come
to an end for all I was concerned. I could not, as one does
with a pet, leave him to his own devices in the expectation
that he would soon adapt himself to his new environment.
The crow whom I had acquired at about the same time
quickly made himself at home to the extent of arousing in
us quite the opposite concern, for he immediately forsook
every article of his corvine inheritance, even speaking in a
ludicrous imitation of the tongues of men, and established
himself in our midst with such bland assurance and dis-

respect that we were at a loss to know how we would ever rid ourselves of his company. Though he occasionally joined the local flocks of crows, it was not as one of them but in the capacity of a superior member of our human world who was pleased to condescend. And he always returned after a few minutes to plague us, landing on our heads from behind, mussing our hair, tweaking our ears, snatching the food from our table, and robbing us of whatever possessions we left lying about loose. Within a few hours of his arrival he had accepted all the privileges of a member of human society, without taking on himself any of the consequent obligations. He acted the part of the self-made man ruthlessly and with complete disregard of the established values that go with breeding. He had no pride of ancestry to restrain him. But Akbar, the aristocrat, would not even meet us halfway; it was up to us to come to him. It was my constant study during those first few weeks to adapt myself to his requirements, first of all by acquiring a small library on falconry and boning up on the subject. I learned all the delicate ways in which a noble hawk must be approached, how to avoid slighting his dignity and ruffling his temper, how I could gradually work myself up in his esteem till I had acquired not only his acceptance but his full confidence. It worked out beautifully on paper, but I found that I needed a good deal more practical experience before I was competent to tackle successfully such a problem as the conquest of Akbar's confidence.

I am sorry to say that I blundered from the start. I shall not go into the details of how I finally got jesses and a bell attached to his legs so that I could keep him in leash. He now had a perch of his own, a wooden sawhorse with the horizontal bar wrapped in layers of sailcloth because the books said he would get sore feet if he stood on wood. He chose to disregard the books, however, if I did not, and habitually perched on the wooden end of the bar in preference to the sailcloth. His ancestors had always stood on wood, and so did he. This alone should have shaken my confidence had I known what it portended. But I had no guidance except for the books; I could look for no other advice.

And the books all stated categorically that the crucial period in the career of a hawk that has been taken from the nest comes while he is "flying at hack." It is essential that the young bird should be allowed to "fly at hack"—that is, that he have his full liberty as soon as he is able to fly. A hawk cannot function successfully unless his education is obtained in the traditional manner of the wild, for he is and must always remain untamed. Otherwise his spirit will be broken, he will become an empty vessel. The young hawk, before he is turned loose, has become accustomed to being fed at a certain hour and a certain place every day. When he is flown at hack he returns to that place at that hour just as naturally as he would otherwise turn to his parents to be fed. But in every other respect he is a wild hawk, and when he shows the first signs of being able to hunt for himself he must be trapped and deprived of his liberty. In the meantime, however, he has had a chance to develop the strength and skill that are his heritage, so that he will prove himself as able and spirited in the field as his brothers in the wilderness.

Akbar took off from the ground on his first flight (at hack) in a style to do credit to his parents and landed among the upper branches of a butternut tree to rest and gather his wits after this initial adventure in freedom. With pride and with misgiving, I contemplated him standing like a bronze eagle on a limb and gazing fiercely at the wide world. He was a sovereign creature now; my only hold over him was economic. With this brave new world before him, this wide dish of forests and fields and lakes all visible from his elevation, would he not be too dazzled to remember his home when, in the evening, he first began to feel hunger? The books said he would not; but my intuition was shrewder. Character is never a sure guide when hunger is in the reckoning, but Akbar's hawkish character was of such superior mettle that I could not easily conceive him stepping out of it. And I was right. Not even under the stress of starvation would he make a concession to my human world. He would not come back. In the afternoon, when I called him to his dinner, he merely stared down at me from his height with the intensity that always characterized his hawkish stare, as if wondering whether I could really be expecting him to descend to my level once more, now that he had successfully risen above it.

The books could not advise me on how to proceed in such a contingency because to have done so would have been to admit that such a contingency could arise. There were two courses open. I could proceed on the assumption that, not having fully realized his freedom yet, Akbar might be taken up without difficulty if I climbed the tree after him. Or I might follow a policy of inaction, hoping that the pressure of hunger would eventually bring him to conform to the established dogmas of the science of falconry. But in the latter case I had to reckon on the increase of his wildness along with that of his hunger. If he had not yet fully realized his freedom, he soon would. When evening came I joined him in the branches of the butternut tree.

There was no moment in the next twenty-four hours that I did not heartily wish I had never committed myself to the pursuit of falconry. No one who had seen Akbar take off from that tree when I joined him in it, sail out into the open sky, and soar aloft in broad circles as though he had been born on the wing, would have blamed me for believing that I had, by my blundering interference, committed a noble hawk to slow and solitary starvation. It was a beautiful and a heart-rending sight to see him rise to his birthright and go sweeping away northward till he had disappeared over the rim of the woods that border Trinity Lake, his jesses streaming behind him as a last reminder of his captivity. I faced the prospect of a week in which I would have always before my mind's eye and deep in my conscience the spectacle of his gradual exhaustion. There seemed little chance that I would ever find him again.

Akbar came back, but he came back a crippled hawk. The evening following his escape, after a day-long and desperate search, he was found high up in an oak that grew in the woods above Trinity Lake and was captured by means of a device which we improvised for the purpose, a pole, some thirty feet long, to the end of which a bent nail had been fastened. Akbar looked down at us with steely eyes as we slowly raised the end, garnished with a hunk of meat, toward his branch and moved it to within reach of his talons. For a moment he was suspicious and crouched for flight. But the meat was tempting. With a stab of his foot he secured it, and then, while he devoured his first meal in forty-eight hours, we caught the bent nail in one of the leather jesses that hung from his talons. In a moment we had jerked him from his perch and dragged him down, while he flapped his great wings furiously against the branches to get free.

The injury that we did Akbar was not immediately apparent on his recapture. Only the next morning, when he tried again to fly from my hand, he suddenly collapsed and hung helplessly at the end of his leash, one wing loose and lifeless. The tendon which ran along its leading edge had been almost severed when he beat against the branches, and now at the first strain it snapped.

The history of Akbar up to this point should have persuaded me that falconry was not a pursuit to be entered upon light-heartedly. It is one thing to keep a tame crow or a tame parrot and quite another to involve oneself with a wild hawk. But just at this point an opportunity arose for me to make a fresh start in falconry, and I accepted the challenge. Not to have done so would have been to abandon the vision that had possessed me during all those weeks since I had watched the mating of Akbar's parents, the vision of a hawk of my own whom I could take out into the fields and fly like a paper kite. The thirst for knowledge prompted my vision, though I cannot claim a properly scientific intention to give it weight. It was more the kind of understanding that the portrait painter gains from the close study of his subject that I was after.

Obviously, I could hope for only a crippled understanding from a crippled hawk. The sight of Akbar's disability, as well as being a constant reproach to me, would seem a mockery of a world that had meaning only in its integrity.

Shelmerdine also came of good raptorial stock, even if he could not claim quite the same sort of antique nobility as Akbar. His dapper parents were at once less fierce and more graceful in their manners, resembling the courtly nobility of the eighteenth century rather than the martial nobility of the crusading Middle Ages—especially the male, in his delicate costume of white and pearl-gray, with his long, flexible wings and rakish tail. The female was larger and more sedate, her brown plumage distinguished only by the flashing white of her upper tail coverts. She seemed altogether a more serious bird.

Their courtship differed from that of the red-shoulders as did their character. The male's approach had nothing dominating or warlike in it. He made his appeal for her consent on purely æsthetic grounds, his wooing, which I observed from the grassy hills beyond Trinity Lake, taking the form of an exquisite sky-dance in which he performed a series of breath-taking acrobatic feats with superb and scornful ease. He would loll over on his back in the sky like a swimmer floating in the sea, then sweep downward head-first in a great circle, which, without a movement of his wings, would carry him up again to his original floating position. He looped the loop repeatedly, without effort and seemingly without power. Occasionally, tiring of the simple repetition, he would come to the ground in a series of slow and continuous barrel-rolls, wing over wing, level out just before he struck the grassy fields, loop, and ascend again with an easy beating of his long wings. In his way, he was proving his superiority as a hunter to the attendant female as effectively as the male red-shoulder a few weeks earlier. For the marsh hawk depends on quickness and agility, rather than speed and power, to capture his prey. His method is to skim just above the surface of swamps and open fields, quartering back and forth over a restricted area till he catches sight of some small mammal or bird in the grass below him, when, with a sudden loop that reverses his direction almost more quickly than the eye can follow, he returns upon it. The formidable ability to charge from a height, which is the red-shoulder's specialty, would be useless to the harrier. He belongs to a different school of aviation.

By the time I had decided to embark on a second venture in falconry I was already familiar with the habits of Shelmerdine's parents, so familiar, in fact, that I knew of his existence and could accurately estimate his age. At first both male and female had been in the custom of coming by our house every day to hunt in the Meadows. When, after a few weeks, the female no longer appeared, I knew she had laid her eggs and was already in confinement. For the domestic economy of the harriers is based on a complete division of labor: the female broods while the male does the hunting, bringing home the family bacon and passing it to her in mid-air near the nest. Soon I noticed that he was always flying north when his talons were loaded. That gave me the direction of the nest. North of our house are two large swamps. If the nest had been in the nearer of the two I would surely have seen the female occasionally when she came out to meet her returning mate. By subtraction, then, I located it in the farther swamp, and there I went. Within thirty seconds I had flushed the sitting female.

Shelmerdine, when I found him on the low platform of broken reeds that served as a nest, was already half-clothed in his immature plumage. He stood looking up at me with a sort of sullen defiance. If he had any brothers or sisters they had escaped into the cattails before I came upon them.

But one hawk was all I wanted, and that evening Shelmerdine came home with me.

The range of individuality among birds is generally overlooked by casual observers. It is true, nevertheless, that no two birds in a flock, when they are acting individually, will respond in exactly the same way to the same prompting. Some will be friendly and some pugnacious; some will be tame and some wild; some will lose their heads at a danger signal, some will not. Separate them from the mob spirit that dominates the flock and it is surprising what variety you will find. Only in his inflexible refusal to suit himself to the environment I offered him was Shelmerdine at all like Akbar; and even there he differed radically, for his stubbornness seemed more that of peevishness than of pride. Akbar always had the high serenity of a being who rises superior to the imperfect conditions of his existence. But Shelmerdine was definitely an unhappy hawk, with the sullen and embittered disposition of a spoiled child. His unhappiness was so evident in his manner that it infected all who went near him and foiled every attempt at friendliness.

My respect for Akbar increased progressively as I became more familiar with Shelmerdine. Even as a fledgling you could never have compared Akbar with a child; only rare human beings, in fact, have such measure of the virtues that characterize an adult. For one thing, no one could think of Akbar so slightingly as to pity him, even when he was starving, or when his injured wing had made a mockery of the independence of his spirit. His dignity was never touched by adversity. But Shelmerdine, sound of wing and well cared for, was always an object of pity. By contrast

with Akbar he represented the petal of an effete aristoc-
racy trembling at every hostile breeze. No cherishing could
reconcile him to the burden of his existence. Whenever I
came within sight of his perch, he began a monotonous and
peevish screaming which always seemed forced, like the
crying of a naughty child trying to draw the attention of
its elders.

The contrast in disposition reflected itself in appearance
as well as manners. Akbar was always statuesque, posing
rigidly erect on his perch, his broad shoulders squared to
the world, his small head set well back, his two eyes piercing
like gimlets whatever they looked at; he was always the
picture of strength in repose. Shelmerdine's appearance,
like his disposition, was restless. More elegantly built, with
a narrow body and long, rakish tail, he leaned forward
and his head was lowered with an air of suspiciousness that
was confirmed in the discontented expression of his eyes.
His wings were firmly set and blended to his body, their
sharp points crossing each other above the rump; while
on Akbar one shoulder hung loose and the corresponding
wing-point stuck out askew from his back. But a glance was
enough to reveal Akbar's innate superiority.

The breaking of my faith with Akbar after his injury,
the acquisition of another bird to take his original place
in my plans, was definitely wrong. Akbar's ancient stamina,
as it proved, rose above such a comparative triviality as a
crippled wing, while the mere burden of ordinary existence
grew altogether too great for the uncrippled Shelmerdine.
As the weeks passed it became evident that the experts I
had consulted were all mistaken in their flat statements that
Akbar's injured wing would never again be of any use to
him. Like other beings of exceptional strength and spirit,

he fooled his doctors by refusing to remain an invalid. He defied science. The process was slow and was never completed, but before the middle of summer he could once more fly; not as he had flown in his one moment of freedom, when his wings had borne him far up into the sky, but on a level course and for limited distances. His wings always remained asymmetrical, the one shoulder depressed below the level of the other and preventing him from rising for any distance. But before his days were over he had proved himself a valiant hunter in contempt of his injury.

The flaw in Shelmerdine was in his spirit and not in his wings. When his flight feathers had as yet attained only half their growth, when his wings still appeared stumpy and incomplete, he was a capable flyer. At first he exercised on the bed of straw that I had given him in substitution for his nest, beating his wing-stumps and leaping repeatedly into the air. His first flight must have surprised him as much as it did me. He jumped from my hand, intending merely to flutter to the ground on his semi-fledged wings; but as he approached the ground obliquely he gained speed, and instead of landing he swept up again toward the tree-tops, flying with ease and buoyancy. In a moment he was lost to sight behind the house. Fortunately his leash was trailing behind him, and when I found him again he was hanging head down from a tall tree at the edge of the woods, screaming for help.

If Shelmerdine's half-fledged wings proved adequate for flight, they became almost too much for him to manage by the time they were fully grown, which was in a very few days. All he had to do was to stretch them, in a yawning, unintentional fashion, and the slightest straying breeze would lift him off his feet. Often he was carried right up to the length of his long leash above his perch and held there like a kite, till he managed his wings so as to sweep backwards and then glide in to a landing, looking invariably surprised and bewildered, as though he had been carried off on a witch-flight against his will. It took him several days to learn that he could not spread his wings in a breeze and still hold his footing.

But where Shelmerdine's wings were more than ample to sustain him, his spirit was not. He never overcame his peevish distrust of life; he never had enough strength of spirit to oppose his own integrity to its pressure. Anything was too much for him, and since he refused to accept life there was no choice left him but to die. I had hoped that he might some day do justice to his parentage by exhibiting in the field the magnificent capabilities with which he was endowed. Instead I buried him, and with no lasting regret, thus closing an experiment that had been marked for failure from the start.

So far two families of hawks had been bereaved by my experiments and I had little to show for it. But birds have not the capacity for mourning or regret as we know it. I doubt that Akbar's parents would have accepted him if I had attempted to replace him forty-eight hours after his theft. I doubt whether they ever had any acute realization of their loss, and I cannot imagine avian anguish. The valor with which birds defend their young seems more an unfeeling response to the practical impulses which nature has imposed on them than a matter of deep parental devotion. To the end of racial survival, and no other, birds are the most practical creatures imaginable. Prompted by the exclusively human emotion of pity, I have drowned a young bird ruthlessly thrown out of its nest by its parents because it happened to be imperfectly formed and thus incapable of carrying on the race.

But there were no imperfections in Akbar's formation when I took him. Of his kind he was the image of perfection, and, on the human plane, that is a good definition of divinity, as divested of its theological trappings. Free from the original sin which makes it impossible for human beings ever to attain the perfection of their kind except in the dreams that inhabit their imaginations and are expressed in the forms of their art, Akbar had every attribute that could be credited to a hawk-god. Whatever had more would thereby be another species of divinity. Of his kind he was perfect. Marring that perfection by my careless blundering was an act of sacrilege tantamount to damaging the image of Pallas Athene in her temple on the Acropolis.

And yet, now that the harm was irrevocably done, Akbar seemed to gain a new nobility from his injury. By that everlasting paradox which makes perfection dependent on imperfection, he became possessed with a suffering grandeur that elevates and enriches his memory in my mind. He had acquired the necessary flaw to make perfection credible. He had transcended his former self as the broken Venus of Milo must transcend the unblemished original. The necessary flaw, the cracked note in the symphony, the drop of wormwood in the nectar, the momentary cowardice of the hero—there you have the secret that gives reality to perfection, that puts it within the grasp of human comprehension. Christ never fully realized his godhead until that moment of doubt on the cross in which he cried out upon his God for having forsaken him. And now, within the lesser scope of his own existence, the perfection of Akbar's selfhood had been completed by its final surpassing imperfection. The broken-winged god was grander and more awful for the touch of ruin.

The remainder of the record is more worthy than the beginning. Akbar was now dependent on my extended hand, whether we liked it or not, and that inescapable fact had its effect on our association. I hesitate to say that in my eyes he became at all pitiful, but the element of compassion was present and lent a warmth to my regard for him which had formerly been lacking. On his side, he seemed to know, in some obscure way, that he had played for his independence and lost. He grew, if not tame, at least more mellow in his acceptance of our relationship. His essential dignity was untouched, he lost none of his reserve. But he was no longer the wild hawk that he had been before his tragedy.

I doubt that I could have kept Akbar for long under other conditions. Sooner or later he would have got away from me and returned to the life for which he was born. I had not the time, and very little of the inclination, to master the delicate and arduous discipline whereby the falconer keeps his hawks on his line, playing upon their hunger to prevent their escaping as a fisherman plays a fish that is only just hooked. It needed this slight injury to make him wholly mine.

But within the limits it imposed Akbar had full scope. Now that circumstances had made him more amenable it did not take long for him to associate my whistle with feeding, and soon I could trust him to come to me when I gave the accepted signal. On a perfectly level course he could not always make it if the distance was great; beating his broad but unbalanced wings in a valiant effort, he would gradually be forced down closer and closer to earth, and often he was obliged to alight short of me and complete the stage on foot, in that half-running, half-hopping gait of his. He always had enough power in his large legs, however, to leap almost vertically to my hand from the ground. When it was a case of starting from a height and descending toward me he was the equal of any sound hawk. On such occasions it took fortitude to face his charge. Most birds, especially those with weak feet, like pigeons and swallows, reduce their speed in alighting by backing their wings hard before they touch. But Akbar belonged to a race of strong-footed hunters whose livelihood depends on the power and speed with which they can strike a solid object. When I called him from his perch in a tree on a hilltop some hundred and fifty yards away, he would start like a shot, beating his wings for the first few seconds to gain momentum, then coast downhill at an accelerating pace, keeping just over the surface of the ground and striking my gloved hand from below without any reduction in his speed, his talons extended straight before him; and since he weighed several pounds, the resounding impact of the blow sent me staggering backward every time. It required a certain amount of skill and quickness, also, to catch him on my glove, for he invariably made to strike the piece of meat in my bare hand directly with both talons. I soon learned to interpose the gloved hand by a rapid last-instant movement to save myself from his claws.

At first Akbar did not engage in any hunting of his own. Though his hunting equipment was fully developed, it was not on the program of a normal avian existence that he should be called on to feed himself before a certain established time had elapsed. Until then, the thought of hunting did not enter his head. If I placed a live frog on the ground below his perch he would fix it with his gimlet eyes in a stare of such intensity that the frog, had it been a more sensitive creature, must have withered up and died on the spot. But starvation itself would not have prompted him to drop on it. The killer instinct had not yet been introduced in this first act of his adolescence. Like the mating and migrating instincts, it remained in abeyance till the proper point had been reached in the drama. This was exclusively the stage of dependence and preparation, the stage that in all animals whose survival depends on their skill is marked by the characteristic juvenile impulse of play. Like the lion-cub or the young gentlemen on the playing fields of Eton, Akbar devoted his novitiate to games of skill intended to develop in him those qualities of strength, agility, and agressiveness which, under normal circumstances, would become essential to his survival.

At the very beginning, a certain bump on the wooden perch that I had erected for him under the butternut tree sufficed for his practice. Eying it with concentrated fury, he would suddenly stab at it with one foot, hold it for a moment in a grip so powerful that his long claws sank into the wood, relinquish it, stab it again. Then he would try the other foot (a hawk must be ambidextrous), and at last he would pounce on it with both feet at once in the final stroke of annihilation. He soon found a better sport, however, in the big yellow butternuts which lay scattered upon the lawn under his perch. It required real skill to subdue these elusive balls. You had to take them unawares, watching them intently with unblinking eyes till the right moment, when, without warning, you fell from your perch like a thunderbolt and transfixed them before they had a chance

to so much as move. What made it especially sporting was
that there were always several within range to be con-
quered. No sooner had you struck one than your attention
was called to its mate lying alongside it, and so you would
be kept busy striking at first one and then the other. It was
amazing what widespread havoc you could wreak in the
colony of butternuts with only two feet, if you were quick
enough. But even after you had caught a couple, they were
likely to get away from you unless you were careful. It was
no joke to maintain your balance with each foot on a rolly
nut. And, of course, you always gave them a sporting chance
for their freedom, the method being to leap into the air
with a captive in your talons, drop him, let him roll a few
inches down the hillside, then overtake and strike him
again in full flight.

By using the word play to describe these exercises I do
not mean to give the impression of playfulness. In Akbar's
case nothing could be falser. He was invariably in fierce
and deadly earnest in everything he did, and no less so in
these sports of his young hawkhood. I never caught any
gleam of humor or frivolity from those eyes. In repose as
in action, in games as in his later conquests of wild animals,
they were always concentrated and terrible. A man with
such eyes would conquer the living earth.

Akbar's first live quarry was a fat old grasshopper we met
on the path leading over the hill toward the Meadows. A
grasshopper was nothing new to Akbar; many before this
one had been impaled on the narrow beam of his eyes and
escaped violence. But today was the day of his confirmation, today for the first time the latent impulses of the
adult hawk rose and took possession of him. Without forethought, without hesitation, giving no warning of the trans-

formation which prompted his intention, he dropped from my hand and struck an innocent clump of grass full in the middle. There was no surprise for me in that. Our walks were habitually interrupted because Akbar felt obliged to attack the sticks and stones that lay in our way. He would stoop from my hand on a broken piece of branch in the path, strike it with both feet, stab at first one end and then the other, maul it, and even roll over on his side, holding the stick clear of the ground in his mock-struggle to subdue it. But this time he struck the clump of grass and remained fixed to it in a stern and immovable attitude, his tail spread against the ground, his long shanks lying flat, his talons squeezing the unprotesting blades with fervor, with determination, with the grip of doom; for this time, in the middle of one tensely convulsed talon, he held the immobilized body of a fat grasshopper, the first victim of his career as a hunter.

The auspicious opening of his career had the effect of making Akbar overconfident at first. For a while he dashed himself at anything that stirred within his range. He never bothered, in this era that was dominated by the memory of his first triumph, to determine the nature of his quarry before he attacked; the impulse was acted upon as it was caused, too quickly for thought. When a woodcock flushed from the grass ahead of us it was as though a string attached to its tail had jerked Akbar from my hand; but the woodcock was off in the distance before he reached the spot from which it rose. Shortly after his first grasshopper, before the Quixotic spirit bred of his original success had given way to the maturer wisdom that comes with failure, he went for a chipmunk and almost caught him under circumstances that would have forestalled a more experienced hawk from ever making the attempt. We were following the path that leads down through the woods into the Meadows when the chipmunk was so ill-advised as to dart across in front of us. Akbar fell from my hand and struck in one movement, grazed his quarry, struck again and missed completely as it dodged into a laurel bush by the side of the path. But he still had a record of repeated successes, and he was not to be foiled by such a stratagem. With a rush he struck the bush in the flank, clearly intending to demolish it at one blow. The chipmunk was so terrified at the attempt that it foolishly darted out from the other side and bounded off down the steep slope of the wooded hillside. Akbar leaped in pursuit, landed on a piece of bark which should have been the chipmunk's tail, and went tumbling head-over-heels down the side of the hill, the bark clutched firmly and triumphantly in his talons, while his intended prize scrambled up a tree to safety.

This was a highly satisfactory contribution to Akbar's education. Having gained confidence in his power, it was well that a measure of disillusion should be poured into his cup to give it the necessary tang of bitterness; knowing something of himself, it was fitting that he should now know the world. How could he properly estimate himself if he underestimated his environment? For the conquest of a tame world would make a poor boast.

In a sense, Akbar's first failure was a test of character. Shelmerdine, under the circumstances, would have sulked and refused to engage himself again in a world that was so retrograde to his desires; almost any man, caught empty-handed after such a display of audacity, would have felt foolish. Akbar did not. He stood on his bit of bark at the bottom of the hill with unruffled composure, so lofty in his

self-possession and so complete in his dignity that any impulse to laugh was cut off in one's throat. You could not
help but take him on the basis of his own self-regard, and
obviously that had not been affected. He was still Akbar,
the serene, the indomitable.

I cannot say what a succession of such failures would have
done to Akbar's character, since he never failed too often
for his own good. Occasionally a grasshopper vanished in
mid-air and left him holding an empty bundle of grass;
but, for the most part, any grasshopper that he singled out
for conquest was as good as dead, any frog that hopped out
from under my feet had hopped his last. The effect of his
few failures was all in the direction of maturity, for by
virtue of them he came to know himself and what was the
proper scope of his endeavors. He learned that grasshop-
pers, toads (if they were not the large garden variety with
the acrid taste), frogs, snakes, and all small mammals who
were so incautious as to venture far from cover, came
within the field of his power, but that birds and squirrels
in the woods were not meant for him. He came to know
the area within which his pride was at stake, the boundaries of his own integrity. To have attempted feats for
which he was not equipped would have been to violate that
integrity; not, perhaps, in the interest of false pride, for
Akbar was only a hawk, but in the interest, at least, of
falsehood. Nature had not intended him for a bird-hawk,
and it would have been a betrayal of his matured self to
have essayed the role once the woodcock's lesson had been
brought home to him. The acquisition of that complete-
ness which is called maturity, in hawks as in men, is, after
all, merely the process of discovering one's selfhood, with

all the possibilities and the limitations that are inherent in the design.

If Akbar soon learned his limitations, he did not realize his possibilities any the less. Granted that he had been crippled in the first of the two outstanding faculties which distinguish birds and give them a superiority over the creatures that crawl upon the surface of the earth, he still had the astonishing power of vision which, when it is known, must be an equal source of wonder in the blinking eyes of men. I would not, in any other context, refer slightingly to our human eyesight; excepting only the birds, no other creatures can boast its like. If we are notable in the animal kingdom for any particular physical capacity it is our vision that makes us so; our other primary senses, those of hearing and smelling, are not nearly so highly developed. The world we know is first of all a world of sights, a world of light and color; the sounds, the odors, the tastes, and the tactile sensations are all of a lesser order. But even in our most highly developed sense we fall far short of the development of birds. With my binoculars to my eyes I could not match the acuteness of Akbar's vision. Those clear and lucid jewels within which all the essential vitality of generations of hawks seemed to be focused into two radiant points of intensity were more than mirrors of the soul; they could accomplish, without the effort of concentration, practical feats that would make a prodigy of a man.

In some respects I was able, on the basis of induction, to re-create in my imagination an image of what those eyes took in. It was evident, for example, that our respective conceptions of distance were totally at variance; which may have been appropriate when you consider that a hawk can

cover a hundred yards in the time it takes me to cover ten,
and will fly from the center of North America to the shores
of the southern continent in the ordinary course of his day-
to-day existence. I recall the first pilgrimage we made to
the scene of Akbar's birth, in the days when we began to go
on these excursions together. At the point where the path
comes out of the woods into the open, Akbar suddenly
shied like a frightened pony, leaping from my hand as if a
paper-bag had been exploded in his ear. At the time I
thought nothing of it, attributing it to some mental vagary
in his over-alert consciousness, but when, on subsequent
walks, the same behavior was repeated at the same point, I
began to take notice. At first I could find no external explanation of his baiting, but finally one day I lighted on the
cause, and subsequent observations confirmed my discovery. On a hillside nearly a quarter of a mile from where the
path emerged from the woods a herd of cows belonging to
a neighboring farmer was usually grazing. Akbar had never
before seen cows, and those great horned beasts that seemed
so far away to me that I had not even noticed them were
close enough to startle him by their proximity.

You see that my education, too, was proceeding. The
history of Akbar and the cows, which I did not credit fully
till I had put it fully to the test, was like a revelation, a sudden insight that increased my understanding of hawks in
general. It made their reactions clearer and more compre-
hensible. I understood now why a wild hawk would not
let me approach closer than about an eighth of a mile in
the open when, according to our different standards, I was
so much closer to him than he was to me. I had taken too
much for granted, when I peered at these hawks through
my field-glasses, trying to make out the markings that dis-

tinguished their species across the distance that separated us, in supposing that they saw me no better than I saw them. For in their eyes I must have appeared as if I had been standing beside them.

In this new light, the lack of ordinary wariness shown by Akbar's younger brother, who now inhabited the Meadows and the fringe of woods about its edge, could almost be characterized as confiding (an expression habitually used with the utmost lack of humor by all bird-annalists). I cannot say he was different in his confidence from any of those other hawks who in the guileless innocence of their youth have not yet learned to guard themselves against the guileful ignorance of men who believe that all hawks are vermin. I single him out because he was Akbar's brother and nest-mate, and because the independence which he had not lost complemented Akbar's career, completing the picture of a whole hawk with the one element which was, perforce, lacking in the circumstances of Akbar's life. Here you had Akbar (I could not for the life of me have told them apart without my captive's dislocated wing and the thongs about his feet), the hawk-god, as he might have been, his body symmetrical, his flight magnificent and careless, his liberty as wide and untrammeled as the serene skies that, during those hot midsummer days, stretched away beyond the reach of the imagination. This was the free Akbar, no less terrible in the stare of those eyes that were immovably fixed to point forward beneath their beetling brows, no less ruthless in the use of those yellow talons, no less inflexible in his adherence to the traditional ways of his ancestors. Knowing both hawks in their day-to-day life, I came finally to know the one hawk-god, who, whether in captivity or in freedom, on the lawn by our house or in the woods that border the Meadows, learned the skill of his vocation by attacking broken twigs and clumps of grass, stood immovably on the body of his prey till its quivering had ceased, tore out shreds of flesh from its warm body with his sharply hooked beak, and perched rigidly for hours at a time, one foot drawn up into the heavy, loose feathers of his belly, his little head occasionally pivoting slightly on his broad shoulders to follow some movement that attracted his attention. I came to know the power and ease of his flight, and the vision, always pointed and alert, like an arrow about to be shot, which annihilated distances beyond my scope.

No demonstrations of recognition or brotherly affection ever marked the meetings of the two Akbars. They took notice of each other, as indeed they took notice of everything that lived and moved within their horizons, by their fixed and mutual stares, but they did not communicate. Both of them were habitual screamers, opening their beaks wide when they were hungry or felt particularly fierce to emit the sharp, high-pitched cries that are among the wildest sounds in nature, but the screams of one never evoked a response from the other. I think they must have understood that under the circumstances in which I had come between them they were not the rivals they would otherwise have been and, having neither common nor opposed interests, were content to disregard whatever bond of brotherhood may have existed between them.

Unlike the crow, whose social requirements made him regard us all as specially appointed by a benign corvine Providence to be his playmates every hour of the day, Akbar had the solitary disposition which was in keeping with the noble independence of his spirit. He was never hostile to me, but it was always clear that he could get along equally well without me. He was quite sufficient to himself. When the crow, having brought us all to the point of nervous prostration, cast about for other partners in his sports and finally, with the terrifying tactlessness of his low breeding, fixed his glittering gray-blue eye on Akbar, the big hawk never for one moment lost the lofty self-command and aloof manners proper to an aristocrat confronted with his inferiors. Before that raucous urchin he seemed to take on added stature, to become the very essence of true nobility. It has been said of the crow (who later passed into the keeping of a friend and had his antics recorded for posterity in a biographical notice published in one of our leading monthlies) that he was completely insensitive to the things of the spirit, that he had, in other words, no soul. Only such flagrant insensitivity, such utter lack of any tact, could have allowed the crow to seek out Akbar as a playmate. I record the fact with a proper sense of all its shocking implications. The crow was too ignoble, too vulgar and small-minded, to appreciate the respect due his betters. He must have had some dim and uncomfortable awareness of Akbar's superiority, however, for he approached him with the loud, defensive quarrelsomeness of a consciously inferior being who wants to show that he's just as good as anyone else. He felt obliged to disguise the unwarrantable friendliness of his intentions.

If you have ever seen a ragamuffin dancing about in the street before a rival of whom he is secretly afraid, holding his fists up in a defensive and threatening attitude, as ready to run as to attack, you have some conception of how the crow danced about on the far end of Akbar's perch. His loud and guttural language, if it could have been translated into human terms, would have been unprintable in such a text as this. He shouted his threats for the world to hear, calling on the hills and the fields to witness his quarrel, while taking great care to keep his distance. Akbar, as became his station, took not the slightest notice. In the perfect composure of his demeanor he gave no sign of hearing the shouted challenges of the crow. He merely stood erect and at ease on his perch, his head well back on his shoulders, his eyes fixed intently on some point in space miles beyond the black figure sparring at his feet. Gradually the crow, incapable by his nature of understanding the big hawk's impassive negligence, became emboldened to dance up closer along the perch, weaving back and forth with his head in an attitude of mock heroics, making threatening passes with his open bill, and shouting in the aggrieved tones of one who is looking for a quarrel but has no plausible excuse to lend it dignity. He was obviously stung by Akbar's insulting disregard of his pretensions, and finally, in desperation of making himself noted, he went too far. Akbar turned his head, fixed him with his eyes, and before there was time to make a move in defense one yellow talon had shot out and caught him firmly by the throat, in the middle of a derisive caw that abruptly fell to a weak, rattling gurgle. For a moment he was shaken helplessly back and forth, like a small boy in the grip of an angry parent, then flung from the perch to land sprawling a half-dozen feet away in the grass, his feathers ruffled, his wings disordered, his feet in the air. Akbar remained erect and impassive as ever while the crow picked himself up, shook out his feathers, and, giving a few plaintive caws which implied that he had been attacked unfairly, without cause and without warning (and which may have contained some threatening reference to a big brother, for all I know), departed in disgrace from the scene of his punishment. I suppose he knew that Akbar could have eaten him then and there, had he cared to, but he could never have understood the spirit of *noblesse oblige* that had saved him.

It was simply not in Akbar to make friends, whether with man or beast. It was not in his breeding, in the distant and lonely grandeur of his kind, to admit the compromises necessary to any intimate association of the sort. Again, as always in nature, there is a strictly practical reason for the solitary independence of hawks. Each hawk needs a wide territory of his own in which to make his living and can brook no rivals on his hunting grounds. Because there can be no profitable communal co-operation among hawks, they remain strict individualists, dividing up the available territory among them like the feudal lords of the Middle Ages, and regarding all trespassers as rivals to their sovereignty. It is probably not uncommon for a hawk to see no other individual of his species from the end of fall to the beginning of the following spring; like Kipling's cat, also a mighty hunter, he hunts by his wild lone. By his very nature the hawk-god is a jealous god.

It was with a jealous eye, then, that Akbar regarded the multitude of hawks that began to parade overhead in early September on their southward migration. He watched them as a feudal lord on the walls of his stronghold might have watched the cavalcade of a rival noble passing along a distant road. But distance here was not measured in human terms. Until that fall I had no conception of the many hawks which migrate at such altitudes that they remain beyond human sight. Only Akbar saw them. Suddenly his gaze would be fixed toward a point just above the northern horizon. I might strain my eyes to their utmost and still see nothing but the empty sky. But slowly, steadily, without relaxing the fixity of his stare, Akbar would follow the invisible point up into the sky, follow it on overhead, and finally, often as much as a quarter-hour later, follow its fall below the southern horizon. A migrant hawk, clear to him while completely beyond my vision, had passed over on his way south. One hawk, or possibly a dozen. Sometimes, pointing my binoculars in the indicated direction, I could make out a little swarm as of particles of dust suspended in the field, slowly circling about each other and floating across space. Other times, binoculars or no binoculars, I could make out nothing. And Akbar not only saw them, he saw them clearly enough to identify them. For he would rarely bother to glance at other birds, and when he did it was only to glance. An airplane might come roaring over, or a crow might swoop across the field of his vision, without attracting his interest; but let any little falcon, however small and however far away, come within the circle of the horizon, and Akbar's stare would follow him unfalteringly till he had gone.

If Akbar was a jealous hawk, he was not necessarily hostile. The episode with the crow had proved the quality of his temper. On his own terms he was always willing to accept the presence of others, if not their intimacy; he stood on his rights and contained himself in serenity so long as they were not infringed. But he knew how to act in the face of a threat. Akbar is out in the middle of the lawn before the house, standing on a bullfrog which he has caught in the vise of his talons, waiting for its last convulsive movements to expire. He stands fiercely erect, looking about him and then down at the frog, his eyes even more flagrant than usual. Suddenly, for no immediately apparent reason, he ruffles up all his feathers and spreads his wings and tail against the ground, crouching low and completely hiding the frog under the tent formed by his body. If you look up you may see the reason in a small rival circling aloft in the sky. Akbar takes no chances. If I came up to him while he was feeding it would be the same thing, and even I, who know him and am trusted, would hesitate to dispute possession of the frog with him before he had, at least partially, satisfied his hunger upon it.

But generally the wild hawks were content to mind their own business as Akbar was to mind his. Only the yearling sharp-shins who had not yet outgrown the games of their youth ever took any notice of him; they found it great sport to stoop on us when we were out for one of our airings, folding their wings and falling from immense heights to clear our heads by a few feet with a sudden, terrible sound of rushing air, like the twang of a harp-string. I always had the impulse to flinch when I saw them coming, but Akbar's stalwart example in remaining unmoved gave me courage to adopt a like attitude. I think any young sharp-shin who had seriously intended to strike would have glanced off the edge of Akbar's dignity without touching either of us.

It was not difficult to conceive of the keenness of Akbar's vision, even if I could not share it; I had merely to imagine how the world would look to me if its distances were cut by half or three-quarters. But in one respect the power of his eyes was completely mysterious: he could look directly and unblinkingly into the sun without being dazzled. He never left off staring at a passage hawk because its course took it across the face of that sphere in which all details were lost to my sight. Directly against the blinding radiance of a summer sun he could see a speck so small that, even when it was out in the blue, it was practically invisible to me. I have been assurred, more than once, that when birds look into the sun they draw up over their eyes those thin, transparent membranes that serve them as inner eyelids, much as a man might raise a smoked glass to dim the brilliance. It simply is not true. For Akbar looked at the sun, invariably, with his naked eyes.

I don't know why men should take such satisfaction in discovering those faculties in which the beasts surpass them. Even when you grant that our confidence in our own superiority allows us to be generous in trifles, you have not explained the positive pleasure we take in finding flaws in that superiority. In the interests of fact, now, I shall have to record that Akbar's vision was, in an incidental respect, inferior to our own. For Akbar, who could face the sun itself without flinching, could not see in the dark half as well as I could. When dusk came and we went together into the dimly lighted garage that was his shelter for the night, I had to place him on his perch as you might place a clock on a mantelpiece, for he could not see it himself. In a light that was still strong enough to give me a fairly clear idea of near-by objects he was a blind hawk.

Another respect in which Akbar could not match my human faculties was more a matter of recognition than of vision itself. He could not, no matter how close it was, identify a motionless object as a living animal to be caught and eaten. Any little beast, though it were out in the open and only a foot away, was perfectly safe as long as it did not move; but let it take one step and it was done for. I have seen Akbar pounce merely at the rustle of a blade of grass and emerge with a shrew that had been completely hidden from sight, but he invariably overlooked the big bullfrogs that sat about the edge of our pond. I had to catch them myself and bring them out on the open lawn for him to take; at the water's edge, however close over them I held him, he would not see them until they had jumped and were gone in the depths of the lake. The fault was definitely a fault of the imagination. Akbar's could not tell him the difference between a motionless frog and a stone; to him, only animation betrayed the animate.

I have said that in the simplicity of his character, in his integrity and independence, Akbar had the shape of an epic hero, expressing perfectly one aspect of the primitive, multiple, and utterly mysterious mother-organism within which our own lives are curled as in the hollow of a hand. His proportions were definitely epic. But as I approach the inglorious end of his career and look back over the frustration of his days, which were never to number over two hundred, I am aware that his story has no epic quality. It is rather the tragic history of a lofty character in a foreign environment against which it is not equipped to defend itself, of an inflexible spirit defeated by circumstances over which it has no control. His is the tragedy of Coriolanus, living in a changing world under conditions that made it impossible for him ever to fulfill his inborn promise, the promise, bred of his quality, that he would be to Rome "as is the osprey to the fish, who takes it by sovereignty of nature." Akbar, like Coriolanus, was an exiled and defeated sovereign. But the inflexible Roman, torn by the conflicts and uncertainties that are the heritage of men, was forced in the end to compromise with the improper world in which he found himself. Akbar, in the immense simplicity and integrity of his hawkish heritage, retained his resolution.

Akbar had risen above and remained untouched by the

ignorance and petty hostility of a crow; the ignorance and the petty hostility of a man destroyed him. That desire to assert oneself by scoring against anything that has the aspect of nobility is common to all of us. I have heard the note of triumph in the voices of men describing the size and beauty of a hawk they have brought to earth, and I know that the destruction of no other bird brings quite the same satisfaction. Few hunters can resist such a trophy. The instinct of vandalism is inherent in us all, but in most cases we have enough self-discipline to control it. Only the tragic error by which men believe that all hawks are vermin allows them to indulge the impulse which is responsible for the slaughter of many thousands every season and their gradual disappearance from the land. It makes no difference that biologists consistently report that the great majority of species, of which Akbar's is one, are predominantly beneficial to the interests of mankind, or that they are protected by law; popular ignorance makes no distinction between species. The petty hostility of a man, unleashed by ignorance, was responsible for Akbar's death.

Since his accident Akbar was no longer kept on a leash and could enjoy what freedom his maimed wing allowed him. Often he would spend hours on a low branch in the woods watching with the accustomed intensity of those sharp eyes the countless forms of small wild-life that inhabited their shelter. One evening during the hunting season, after a day in which the usual quiet of the countryside had been disturbed by the continual explosions of guns, I could not find him. I never saw any sign of him again. The hunter who brought him down, seeing the jesses about his legs, took good care not to leave any tell-tale traces behind him. I hope that when he held the limp body up—by the feet, I suppose, its head hanging loose like a heavy tassel at the end of a cord, its eyes glazed and without character— his triumph was at least tinged with shame. Such a trophy should have had a greater end.

BIRDS AGAINST THE SEA

Birds against the Sea

I

"THE first time I ever saw an albatross," wrote William Beebe, "was at dawn far out in the Indian Ocean." That simple statement, read at a time when I had been confined to city-life for longer than was good, inaugurated my interest in birds. Far out in the Indian Ocean—dawn—the first albatross! Then and there an inner revolt took place. I had followed Dr. Beebe and his crew of scientific adventurers out of New York Harbor in the *Arcturus*, past Cape Hatteras, through the Sargasso Sea, through the Panama Canal, and right onto the Equator, without being more moved than becomes an arm-chair adventurer who can always retire at a moment's notice to the comfort and security of a book-lined study. But, without knowing it, I had been sailing dangerously close to the brink—and then that burning dawn (I am sure the dawn is redder in the Indian Ocean than elsewhere), that albatross, were enough to push me over.

"It was that hour at sea when perspective does not exist, and, like the houses of a tropical coastal city, everything appears flat and on one plane. I was observing a small flock of petrels from the rail of my vessel when a lighter-colored bird appeared above them, apparently of the same size. As I watched, it grew larger and larger, until, to my amazement it joined the petrels, and in the same instant they were

dwarfed to insect size while this white bird assumed relatively gigantic proportions, and I knew that I was seeing
the effortless flight of an albatross." If I had enlisted for
the sea on the moment no one but Dr. Beebe would have
been responsible, and he has much to answer for in my subsequent career. The interest engendered by his albatross
grew rapidly, until, to my amazement, it assumed relatively
gigantic proportions. I took off from the pages of ornithological handbooks and ranged all seven seas on the tireless
wings of the rovers, sometimes drifting on a warm breeze
through tropical archipelagoes, sometimes balancing with
superb ease in the teeth of a westerly along the Roaring
Forties, and again winging my way from the Arctic to the
Antarctic in two lines of print.

II

It is some consolation, if you are as much troubled over
the increasing subjection of nature by man as over the
subjection of man by nature, to reflect that two-thirds of
the globe's surface remains an unconquerable wilderness.
By a welcome paradox, the sea, in which all is drift and
continual change, is nevertheless the most abiding feature
of the earth. It is still the sea of Genesis. The American
continents have been so scarred in the past four and a
half centuries that the contemporaries of Columbus would
hardly recognize them if they returned, but the ocean they
crossed would give them no clue to the lapse of time. The
waves roll over and obliterate the furrows men plow on its
surface.

The peregrinations of the birds that inhabit this wilderness are not only more extensive, but also more improbable,
than those of land birds. They constitute a problem that

science has failed to solve. It is easy to believe that land-
marks play some part in guiding land birds on their trans-
continental migrations, but where are the seamarks that
guide the overseas contingents? A familiar story tells of the
Indian traversing the ocean on his first voyage in a white
man's ship who spent all his time in the forepeak scrutiniz-
ing the waves ahead, till finally he had to admit himself
defeated: he could not see the trail the white man followed.
Of course we know that the trail was as plain as the nose on
his face; only it was marked, not on the sea itself, but on
a chart that reproduced the sea in miniature, and the eyes
of the white man took the form of compass and sextant.
With regard to the navigation of birds we are all of us,
including our ablest pathfinders and medicine-men, in the
position of that wondering Indian.

If it were merely a matter of direction, the problem would
be simpler. We might, however ridiculous it sounds, suppose that birds carry their compasses around in their heads,
that the earth's magnetic poles affect their brains so they
can tell north from south and east from west. But that
would still leave their navigation only partly explained,
and we would finally have to add charts and sextants to the
supposed furnishings of their craniums. For birds, in addition to a sense of direction, have a sense of location so ac-
curate that one could believe them capable of seeing the
entire surface of the globe, with all its islands and continents, in one panorama. They behave as if their vision were
not bound at all by our horizons. The golden plover that
leaves the coast of Alaska sets its course over the ocean in a
straight line for the Hawaiian Islands, two thousand miles
below the horizon and hardly bigger than a grain of sand on
the sea. Terns that have been taken from their island nest-

ing grounds, drugged, and transported across a thousand miles into waters outside their normal range, have returned to their nests within a few days of being released.

Because the sea areas of the globe are so much more extensive than the land areas it is natural that the sea birds should be the most extensive wanderers of all. Though no ornithologist has ever been able to accompany a sea bird on its travels for more than a few days at a stretch (and then only when the bird was accompanying the ornithologist's ship), one may reasonably suppose that individuals have been circumnavigating the globe since thousands of centuries before a member of Magellan's crew became the first man to follow suit. A wandering albatross was shot by a French sea-captain off the Horn at a season when it should, by all the rules, have been nesting at Kerguelen Island on the other side of the globe. Take that into consideration with the fact that mated albatrosses often relieve each other on the nest only at intervals of a week or more and you have grounds for wondering whether it was circumnavigating the globe during one of those intervals. Another albatross, shot off the coast of Chile, bore a vial about its neck with a note from a whaler, dated twelve days earlier and over three and a half thousand miles away in the South Seas.

III

The wandering albatross, I learned from my handbooks, belongs to an order of birds (Procellariiformes) that enjoys a doubly distinguished position in the class Aves. First: it is the most pelagic order, most of its members ranging the high seas quite independently of coastlines. Second: it exhibits the greatest diversity of size, possibly, in the entire animal kingdom, from the Wanderer himself, largest of flying fowl, through the middle-sized fulmars, petrels, and shearwaters, to the swallow-sized diving and storm petrels. These two factors alone, the lording of the group over the wildest habitat and the variety of its members, would have been enough to explain its attraction for one who had never before taken an interest in birds. But there was a third factor that weighed with the other two. These birds represented distance, and in my mood at the time distance was what I wanted above all else. The fact that the majority, and those the most spectacular, occurred in the high latitudes of the southern hemisphere, as far as possible from the world I knew, gave a freedom to my imagination that it could not have had in regard to birds that range along familiar shores. I was more romantic then. Before I could tell a warbler from a sparrow in my own backyard I had a fair knowledge of the sea birds of the Antipodes, and I could probably have identified a pintado petrel (Cape pigeon) at sight.

One might say of my early wanderings that they all had, for their magnetic center, the South Pole. There was more reason in this than the mere distance accounts for. Since the southern hemisphere is largely one continuous ocean, in contrast to the land hemisphere of the north, it has by far the most abundant assortment of open-water fowl that is to be found on the globe. "In the 'roaring forties,' " wrote Alexander in his *Birds of the Ocean,* "on the voyage from the Cape of Good Hope to Australia or on a voyage to or from New Zealand round Cape Horn the ornithologist will probably see daily nearly as many species of sea-birds as he would see land-birds in a country walk at home. . . . Some will follow the ship, beating to and fro across the stern. . . . Others . . . will be seen flying rapidly over the surface of the water, skimming over the crests and disappearing in the troughs." Albatrosses and prions, mutton birds, fulmars, skuas; giant, great-winged Kerguelen, soft-plumaged, white-chinned, white-headed, pintado, and blue petrels; terns and sheath-bills—they skimmed the waves, fluttered in the troughs, beat up against the wind, soared and plunged over the unbroken ocean of the far south. Their wild screams reached me faintly through the pages of those fortunate travelers who had sailed their seas.

I began, also, to follow the seasonal movements of the penguins, birds that one unversed in ornithological science might mistake for the monstrous progeny of some illicit relation with seals. But the penguins are not far removed from the petrel group, though the latter numbers in its ranks the greatest flyers of the animal kingdom, and a voracious seal is their chief enemy. The wings of penguins, which probably bore their ancestors through the air in proper avian style, have become adapted to nothing better than underwater flying, and if one supposes that they find their way about the trackless oceans by some sort of super-sight, then one has to explain away the fact of their myopia, which again seems more appropriate to seals. The penguins go the petrels one better in being exclusive to the southern hemisphere; although one genus, following the Humboldt Current up the coast of South America, finds itself straddling the Equator. The emperor penguin, however, is confined to the ice-bound shores of the Antarctic continent, where he nests and rears his young during the long night of the Antarctic winter in a temperature that reaches −80 degrees Fahrenheit and never gets above zero. When summer comes, the families, including chicks too young to take to the water, embark on floating cakes of ice and ride away to the north, migrating on rafts especially provided, as it would seem, by an indulgent nature. But romance is chilled at this point and retreats.

IV

From the inhospitable waters of the southern hemisphere my book-conducted flights carried me northward into the blue oceans that lie beneath the equatorial sun. One might suppose that in the tropics, where the luxuriance of every sort of life is notorious, I would have found sea birds in unparalleled profusion. Not at all. "One may travel for days across the tropical oceans," wrote Alexander, "and see no birds at all, or only an occasional Booby, Bo'sun-bird, or Man-o'-war Hawk, a few Petrels, or a flock of Terns." In tropical seas where birds are common you can be reasonably certain that land is not far off. Of the pelicans, cormorants, man-o'-war birds, boobies, and tropic-birds, which make up the Pelecaniformes, an order as characteristic of tropical regions as the petrels are of the southern hemisphere, only the last-named could be considered fully pelagic. Pelicans and cormorants are as likely to be seen far inland as far offshore, man-o'-war birds are rarely found beyond easy flying distance of land, and boobies, though they are often noted far at sea, always range with reference to the coastlines.

On September 29, 1492, the mariners of the *Niña,* the *Pinta,* and the *Santa María* saw their first man-o'-war and so were encouraged to continue the quest which resulted in the discovery of America. "Saw a bird called *Rabihorcado,*" Las Casas wrote in his abstract of Columbus's Journal, "which forces the pelicans to disgorge what they have swallowed, and then devours it; this is its only way of providing

food; it is a marine bird but never alights at sea, nor goes
twenty leagues from land." Even today the Latin Ameri-
cans refer to the man-o'-war as *rabihorcado* or *horcarabio,*
a combination of two words, meaning "frenzy" and "gal-
lows," which stems from a legend that the bird habitually
commits suicide in a fit of rage by hanging himself from the
crotch of a tree.

It seems strange that a bird so spectacular in appearance,
flight, and habits, which is, besides, known along all tropical coasts and is common to our southern shores, should
have remained an anonymous figure in popular lore. Everyone knows the albatross, if only by name, and that is a testi-
monial to the power of one poet, utilizing a familiar legend
of the sea, to stir the popular imagination; for no one who
has not traveled deep into the southern hemisphere has
ever seen him in life. The man-o'-war, himself the subject
of legend, is known only to sailors and the inhabitants of
tropical ports. His appearances in literature are usually
cloaked with anonymity. "High in the colourless sunshine,"
wrote Conrad, describing a scene off the shore of Borneo,
"a solitary bird, all black, hovered, dropping and soaring
above the same spot with a slight rocking motion of the
wings"; and no one familiar with sea birds could fail to
recognize the description. Better known is the account of
the "sky-hawk" that went down with the *Pequod* and her
crew in the China Sea at the conclusion of *Moby Dick,*
in the scene where the harpooneer, Tashtego, nails the flag
to the descending mast. "A sky-hawk that tauntingly had
followed the main-truck downwards from its natural home
among the stars, pecking at the flag, and incommoding
Tashtego there; this bird now chanced to intercept its

broad fluttering wing between the hammer and the wood; and simultaneously feeling that ethereal thrill, the submerged savage beneath, in his death-gasp, kept his hammer frozen there; and so the bird of heaven, with archangelic shrieks, and his imperial beak thrust upwards, and his whole captive form folded in the flag of Ahab, went down with his ship, which, like Satan, would not sink to hell till she had dragged a living part of heaven along with her, and helmeted herself with it." The "archangelic shrieks" originated in Melville's imagination, for the bird he describes is undoubtedly the silent man-o'-war. Murphy, in his monumental *Oceanic Birds of South America,* confirms the fact that man-o'-wars have been observed, on more than one occasion, obstinately attempting to tear the pennants from the mastheads of ships at sea. But the noted illustrator of a recent popular edition of *Moby Dick* represented the heavenly victim of the scene as an American eagle, the last bird you would expect to find in the China Sea.

Since the *Pequod* and her defiant crew were so obviously bound for hell, it suited Melville to describe his "sky-hawk," by contrast, as "a living part of heaven." He had better have chosen a tropic-bird, or one of the albatrosses; for a more sinister figure than the man-o'-war does not fly the seas. But Melville, in his peculiar imagination, conceived of white, rather than black, as a symbol of the sinister, so perhaps he had some justification in applying the converse. "Bethink thee of the albatross," he wrote, "whence come those clouds of spiritual wonderment and pale dread, in which that white phantom sails in all imaginations?" The answer is, of course, its whiteness. A foolish consistency, however, was never the hobgoblin of Melville's mind, and in another few lines we find the albatross landed in Heaven, amid "the wing-folding, the invoking, and adoring cherubim!"

If Satan should ever choose to incarnate himself as a bird he would find the man-o'-war cut to his measure. The power and beauty of his flight, his predatory habits, and his somber appearance are definitely satanic in the impression they make on the beholder. The first man-o'-war I saw, when at last I had my chance to travel, was all alone in a seascape that might have been designed to frame him. It was evening at the entrance to the Caribbean, and though we had just passed, at a great distance, one tropical islet, no land was in view. As often happens when the sun is low, the horizon showed like a dark thread separating the sea from the sky. Some few clouds were reflected in a silver sheen over large areas of water across which leaden bars traveled in serene and endless succession. The clear sky, the binding line of the horizon, the slumbering ocean, lent an air of suspense to the evening. It seemed to be ready and waiting for some act of creation. Then I looked up and saw him for the first time. At the very center of the picture, directly ahead, the great bird hung motionless, his wings crooked at the shoulders, his tail extended like a pikestaff, his rapacious beak turning from side to side without in the least disturbing the perfect equilibrium of the body.

I had been alert for the pirate all day, knowing that our ship was entering his waters, and here he was upon us as though he had taken the sky at one stroke of his wings. And he was simply gigantic. Having already familiarized myself with his person in the handbooks I should have been better prepared for his black immensity, but this apparition was totally unlooked for. He was the one dark, solid object between unbroken sea and unbroken sky; the whole setting seemed to reflect the majesty and dominion of his presence. It was impossible to doubt that the bird was a pirate. Seeing him for the first time I knew the quick thrill that every law-abiding mariner must feel when he first sees the approaching sail of a ship he knows to be outside the law. But our steam-propelled vessel, with that inhuman purposefulness of the machine moving in blind obedience to inhuman law, forged straight ahead through the sea till her fore-peak was almost under the spread of the outlaw's wings. He hung over us like a fixture in the sky, his long, floating pinions resting loosely on the wind. Only the bony beak swung as the head moved to watch us. Having seen, the wings struck down, the body was jarred forward and began rocking to the strokes that followed in rhythmic succession. A moment later my first man-o'-war had diminished to a black speck in the eye of the setting sun.

One has to be especially careful, for fear of the moralists, in applying the term "noble" to a creature with such a predatory bent. Depending on how much moralism enters into your observation, the man-o'-war will seem either the noblest or most ignoble of birds. It will do no good to argue that in nature there is no such thing as morality, for if there is no morality neither is there nobility. You cannot have it both ways. At bottom there are only the raw facts, which human predispositions may color for human consumption but cannot alter. The fact is that the man-o'-war, being stronger, swifter, and more agile than other birds, makes part of his living by plundering them. That is neither noble nor vicious; it merely illustrates the relative positions of the strong and the weak in the kingdom of nature, without implying anything. Even his victims accept the fact in the utterly unphilosophical spirit that we think of as philosophical acceptance. The red-footed boobies, despoiled on their hunting grounds, share their nesting grounds in complete amity with the dark despoiler.

If we may not judge the man-o'-war's piratical habits, we may nevertheless indulge our sportsmanlike appreciation of fine performance, just as we may admire a great general's tactics without espousing his cause. On first impression this gigantically winged bird would seem to be an example of overspecialization in nature. In this he has gone to the opposite extreme from the penguin, who lost his ability to take to the air in acquiring mastery of oceanic depths. The man-o'-war has the greatest wing area in proportion to his weight of any bird, just as the penguin has the least; and where the penguin is incapable of supporting himself on air, the man-o'-war is helpless except in the air. He cannot swim, he cannot submerge, and his almost rudimentary feet are incapable of bearing his weight on land. Compared with even such specialists in flight as the gulls, the difference in specialization is enormous. The great black-backed gull of our Atlantic coast, with a body of equal size, has a wingspread that is shorter by more than two feet and a tail less than half as long, while his feet must be fully three times larger. To gather just how great the disproportion is between wings and feet in the man-o'-war, one might try to picture a bird that combined the feet of a spotted sandpiper with the wingspread of a bald eagle—but the eagle's spread would still be short by a full foot.

This high degree of specialization is chiefly responsible for the man-o'-war's striking appearance. In the air he gives the impression of one of those fantastic flying machines,

such as Goya pictured, with a little body suspended between enormous and unwieldy sails. Until he manipulates
those sails they appear as an actual embarrassment to him.
I have never seen them stretched out to their full length,
but always loosely held and partially folded, with a sharp
crook at each shoulder. In action they saw the air with a
wide threshing motion and the slender body hanging between is rocked like a little boat. The flight is not graceful
by comparison with that of such a virtuoso as the swallow-
tailed kite, but it is incomparable in its flexibility and
power, and capable of spectacular bursts of speed. The
boobies, who skim the waves like living arrows, are helpless
before the pirate's onslaught; they must either disgorge
their booty or take the chance of being crippled by a slashing stroke of his beak.

The long tail of the man-o'-war, which constitutes almost
half his length, is unfolded only for special maneuvers. In
ordinary flight, whether floating in the wind, soaring, or
flapping, it extends from the body like a bayonet. You see
a man-o'-war hanging in the sky motionless, as a spider
hangs from its thread, tail projecting stiffly, wings floating
wide, when suddenly the figure collapses, overturns, hurtles
downwards with sails askew, like an enormous plane that
has gone out of control—just when you expect the crash,
the tail spreads out, the plunge is abruptly arrested, and as
its beak rakes the water the figure sweeps up into the sky
again, a flying-fish twisting between its mandibles and not
a feather wet. An albatross could not have done that. It
would have had to land on the water first (which is something the man-o'-war could not have done) to have fed
from a resting position. For the albatross, with even greater
sweep and momentum in straightaway flight, has no swal-

low-tail to apply as a brake when he wants to reverse his direction.

Using his tail for a rudder, the man-o'-war can twist and double as adroitly as any flycatcher. I have seen him chasing laughing gulls in a tropical harbor, his tail spread wide to match every dodge of his quarry, which were helpless to shake him off. Again I have seen man-o'-wars playing among themselves like colts at pasture, galloping over the sky with tremendous wing-strides, tumbling, swooping, and side-slipping in pursuit of each other with an agility that would have done credit to swallows. But I have also caught a man-o'-war in my hands because he was unable to take flight from a low perch without a wind to lift him. It was the price he had to pay for the overdeveloped wings that gave him mastery of the sky.

You could almost state it as a mathematical equation that the longer the wings of a bird in proportion to its size, the greater its difficulty in launching itself into the air. Of course, bulk has something to do with it; you could not apply your equation to such little birds as swallows and terns. Among the larger species the short-wings can take off with considerable dash but are incapable of the easy sustaining flight of the long-wings; the long-wings, once aloft, are beyond compare, but they launch themselves with difficulty. Our ring-necked pheasant, whose wingspread is shorter than his length, can rise from the ground like a rocket but must come down as soon, for his flight requires an exertion that he cannot prolong. The man-o'-war, with a wingspread more than double his length, cannot take off at all from the level ground except in the teeth of half a gale, though once aloft he is at ease in any weather.

V

The albatrosses and penguins that first stirred my interest were too far away for me to hope that I would ever see them. The man-o'-war, and his associate species in the order Pelecaniformes, came nearer home. Though his habitual range is within the tropics, the man-o'-war's wings are easily adequate to such a slight excursion as may bring him to our temperate shores. I found records of his casual appearances all the way up the Atlantic seaboard to Nova Scotia and Quebec. The brown pelican, brown booby, and yellow-billed tropic-bird had likewise, at one time or another, turned up as far north as the coast of New England. The wide-ranging habits of the sea birds put even these exotic species within my reach.

It was at this stage, then, that I borrowed a pair of binoculars and began to pay attention to the North Atlantic. Once more in temperate waters, the manuals showed a great increase in the number of sea birds over what had obtained in the tropics. And here, for once, I could observe their flight at first hand.

All the large, long-winged birds are to some extent dependent on a wind for their buoyancy in the air. The flight of a goose, with its meager wings, is much the same regardless of wind; the flight of a gull in a gale differs radically from its flight in a calm. The action of the goose's wings creates the conditions necessary for its support; a large gull, or a man-o'-war, or an albatross, merely offers its wings as passive agents to the wind that bears it aloft. The difference is fundamental, as is the difference between an airplane which moves by its own power and a glider which takes

advantage of extraneous currents of air. A turkey vulture
or an albatross may be becalmed indefinitely, like any sailing vessel, resting on a perch or in the water until a change
of weather restores its motive power. If forced to take flight
it imitates the technique of the goose by beating its wings,
but with an effort that is greater by as much as its wings
are longer. The beauty of the long-wings is in their subtle
adaptations to the currents of air that play upon them, and
while this rarely gives the impression of force, which is so
inspiring in the flight of geese, it makes the bird seem of a
piece with the wind in a perfect balance between the in-
ertia of the living body and the energy of its environment.
The goose transcends the law of gravity by mortal effort;
the other allows itself to be played on by the wind with an
effortlessness that gives its flight an air of spiritual tran-
scendence, something of the supernal quality that must
invest the music of the Æolian harp.

The man-o'-war has so much excess wing surface that he
can afford to hold his wings carelessly, allowing them to
rest at ease on the wind. Other sea birds with narrower
wings, like the shearwaters, albatrosses, gannets, and
boobies, habitually extend them rigidly, monoplane fashion, and meet any variations in the wind by tilting the whole
body to conform. The gulls, with their relatively short,
broad wings, are more flexible and, consequently, more
graceful in flight, though they lack the power and mastery
of the others. The way of a gull in the air is not the way of
an eagle, nor of an albatross. Its wings are continually shift-
ing and swaying and dipping, if ever so slightly, in answer
to the changing gusts. The balance of the body is never
quite certain; it must be varied to meet every variation in
the current of air that supports it. Consequently a gull's

relation to the wind is more intimate than that of some stronger flyers, its response is subtler.

Like most laymen in our part of the world, I had been in the habit of grouping all long-winged sea birds as seagulls, just as an inhabitant of Tierra del Fuego might conceivably think all sea birds petrels. For the order Charadriiformes, to which the gulls belong, occupies a position in the northern hemisphere that is roughly equivalent to the position of the Procellariiformes in the southern. Perhaps I should say that it is, rather, equivalent to the twin orders of petrels and penguins together, for it includes, besides the gulls and terns and shorebirds, the flightless great auk of other days, original possessor of the name of penguin, whose striking resemblance to the southern swimmers caused the later confusion of nomenclature.

The initial step in mastering the subject of gulls, I found, was to learn never to call them "seagulls." To do so betrayed one's ornithological illiteracy and violated the canons of good form. There is no such thing as a landgull, though gulls occur inland; consequently there is no such thing as a seagull. One might as well talk about sea-albatrosses, or landsparrows. The next step, as in any science, was to begin multiplying distinctions. There was no such thing as just a gull. It had to be some sort of gull: a herring gull, or a kelp gull, or a laughing gull, or a silver gull, or a kittiwake. Where at the beginning I had thought of all sea birds as belonging to the one inclusive category of "seagull," I soon learned not only to eliminate the majority but to break up the category itself into innumerable distinctions of genus, species, and race. The handbooks told me of twenty-three species of gulls that have been recorded in North America alone, from the great black-backed gull, almost as large as an eagle, to the little gull, which is hardly larger than a robin.

The gulls are noted for the beauty of their flight; but the beauty of their voices has been generally overlooked. As singers, few if any of our songbirds surpass the best of them. The herring gull's piercing cry has the melodious fullness and smoothness that seduces us in the song of the wood-thrush, with, in addition, an emotional evocative power that the latter virtuoso, for all his bravura, cannot match. Our finest songbirds, as the mockingbird and the wood-thrush, appeal to us by the elaboration and technical fluency of their songs, but whatever emotion they seem to convey is usually only an association with their habitual setting. The song of the woodthrush seems full of melancholy because it is heard chiefly at evening in the dark of the woods. But when you see the actual bird puffing out his throat from the high branch of a tree you feel that he is expressing only the careless enjoyment of the accomplished technician in his skill, giving voice to an undifferentiated animal vitality disciplined by his considerable art. The herring gull's wild cries, besides evoking all our mental associations with the wind and the ocean, have a depth of plaintiveness in their dying out and re-echoing formlessness that might, on occasion, almost move one to tears.

Side by side with the gulls are the terns, a sub-division of the same family. The terns are, most of them, too small for the gliding flight that the larger gulls indulge in, and their style in the air, a quick, continual snapping of the wings, more closely resembles that of the falcons. The wings are never fully spread, in the manner of gulls, but partially drawn in with the points raking back for greater dexterity. The terns are more aerial than the gulls in their structure and habits, however, having relatively small feet, long wings, and a disinclination to put down on the water.

The first tern I recall having seen came in to a landing on a pier along the shore of Buzzard's Bay, where I was embarking for a few days' vacation on the sea. The bird hung over a post in a gale of wind, its coral-red feet reaching for the firm landing. Poised precariously, it held for a moment with wings upstretched, feeling the firmness of wood, then the wind picked it up and whisked it out to sea again. Along the south shore of Nantucket more terns were hunting in the gigantic surf that momentarily roared up and overwhelmed the beach. They faced into the wind, beating their wings, and, when they sighted their prey, dove directly like meteors falling into the sea, disappeared in a little splash of water, and emerged in full flight an instant later, usually with a convulsive silver splinter in their beaks. Along the inner edge of the beach, where the sand was clean and dry above an irregular line of flotsam, they rested on their bellies as if they had no feet at all, creeping forward occasionally like beetles, or like those toy animals that move on hidden wheels. I found the prints of their little webbed feet in double rows, each print overlapping the one before it. When we came among them they rose straight up into the wind, shrieking with anger, and hovered over our heads, dropping down as close as they dared.

The most abundant sea bird of the tropics is also, to me, the most attractive of the terns. Your ship is plowing slowly through a blue enamel sea that appears listless with the heat. A faint haze softens the unbroken ring of the horizon, and the sunlight is so fierce that you seek whatever shade you can find under deck-awnings in which to doze away the hours until evening shall bring relief. The sea appears empty in its whole expanse, for you are now in the hot tropical waters where birds are scarce. Occasionally you open your eyes to the sunlight for a moment to confirm its emptiness. A black speck in the middle distance catches your eye and vanishes. As soon as your vision becomes accustomed to the range you see not one speck but three, four, and then hundreds against the uptilted rim of the sea. At one place they are concentrated like a fog of insects that thins and thickens as they shift position. They all appear to be hovering close to the surface of the water, and as they move, you catch sparkling flashes of the white foreheads and underparts of sooty terns. Then the flock thins out rapidly, scatters, and in a moment you are looking for it in vain.

The sooty terns are among the most pelagic of their family and, at the same time, are the most aerial. Like the man-o'-wars they neither swim nor dive, and it is somewhat of a mystery how they rest at night in the open sea. But almost nothing is known of their pelagic excursions. "However considered," writes Murphy, "it is almost incomprehensible that *millions* of conspicuous, black and white terns, which do not perch, which are incapable of swimming without becoming sodden, which are unresting—flying perhaps for days and days on end—should be almost unreported, swallowed up in the immensity of the Atlantic."

It is a mystery that applies to many birds which do not habitually rest on the water but nevertheless range over the open seas. No one knows how the golden plovers rest on their flights to Hawaii over the Pacific or from Nova Scotia to the West Indies, or if they rest at all. The mystery applies to the arctic terns, which fly down the Atlantic lane between the Old World and the New from the arctic regions to the antarctic and back. If they do rest, there is only one plausible explanation, at least for such a bird as the sooty tern, which cannot sit on the water without quickly becoming waterlogged to the point of helplessness. Voyaging through the open Caribbean I have frequently seen one sooty tern, or two or three, apparently standing on the surface, rising and falling with the waves. The sight is uncanny until you realize that the bird must be perched on some unseen bit of flotsam. Murphy, while he questions that the sooty tern commonly perches at sea, says that the noddy, another tern of the tropics, habitually does, occasionally even using the head of a swimming pelican as a perch.

VI

Measured in terms of its extremes, the long-winged swimmers to which the gulls and terns belong have the most extensive range of any group. Both the northernmost and southernmost records are theirs, the former held by the ivory gull, which has been seen at five degrees from the North Pole, the latter by the great skua of the Antarctic, which has been recorded at between five and six degrees from the South Pole. It may eventually be determined that the skua contributes another record in being the only species of bird to breed in the vicinity of both poles (at present it is a question whether the arctic and antarctic forms of skua are distinct species or merely racial varieties of one common species). In addition, the longest migration known is that of the arctic tern, whose annual distance probably exceeds twenty thousand miles, or almost the circumference of the earth.

Skuas and jaegers, which form a family closely related to the gulls and terns, are predators of the sea, and as such among the fiercest of birds. The skuas are large, dark, powerful, and ruthless. They prey on birds and small mammals, and do not scruple to practice cannibalism on any of their kind too weak to defend themselves. Even the shepherds and sheep-dogs of the Falkland Islands are not safe from their attacks during the nesting season. The jaegers are smaller and not so powerful, with something of the agile, dashing manner of the falcons. I have rarely seen jaegers within sight of land, but I have often watched them at close range from the stern of a ship, beating back and forth like gulls but with greater tautness to their forms, more snap to their wings, and a machine-like efficiency that the gulls lack. Whenever the ship left appetizing morsels in her wake, the little jaegers had first choice and the big herring gulls always gave way to them.

VII

The variety of the order Charadriiformes is attested by the fact that it includes, besides such aviators as the gulls, the large group of alcids, or auks, birds that bear a striking resemblance to the flightless penguins and the almost flightless diving petrels of the south. Murphy, comparing an auk with a diving petrel, to which it is totally unrelated, writes that "the homoplastic resemblance . . . constitutes one of the best examples of convergent evolution known among vertebrates." In other words, starting from dissimilar ancestors and becoming adapted in the course of evolution to similar ways of life, the two birds have gradually achieved an almost unique similarity in their outward forms.

The auks are exclusive to the north as the penguins are to the south. The torrid belt of the tropics separates their ranges. The fascination that the auks exercised on me, almost from the beginning of my interest in birds, was the fascination of bleak northern waters, where the sky and the sea are always gray, where fog and frost share dominion. Like the albatross wheeling over the Indian Ocean, they belonged to a world that was not man's world. When, in the course of a November storm that lashed the Atlantic seaboard, hundreds of dovekies—an auklet no larger than a robin—were scattered over New York City by the wind, falling like rain in backyards and on the flat roofs of apartment-houses, they came as a visitation from outer darkness, reminders of a realm beyond man's dominion. Many of those birds may have had their first close-range experience of man on the streets of Manhattan where they fell exhausted.

Spread out below the high bluffs of Montauk Point, one January, the white-flecked carpet of the ocean was blanketed by dark patches covering acres of its surface where thousands of sea-ducks were bedded down. Sometimes a part of the horizon was completely obscured by smoky masses of ducks flying to their feeding grounds. Loons and grebes floated in the surf that pounded up against the overhanging wall. Clouds of gulls hung in the cold wind that whipped in from the open sea. A gannet, like an immense white flying cross, was putting out to sea in the distance, skimming low over the waves to escape the full force of the wind against him. Two of us stood on the bluffs like ancient mariners, taking turns at a spyglass through which we searched for rare northern species in the great rafts of swimming ducks.

I saw the alcid first out of the corner of my free eye. A wedge-shaped projectile, like a flying penguin, white underneath and black above, he was rounding the point just above the surf, his wings blurred by the rapidity of their strokes. We both got a quick look and then he was gone before we had a chance to identify him. Later in the day, at another portion of the bluffs, we looked down on two alcids bobbing up and down like corks in the high surf, one alongside and a bit behind the other. With their little heads set in close against their bodies and their black-and-white penguin plumage they did not seem like live birds at all, but rather like freshly painted decoys. They rode high on the crashing combers as if at anchor, holding their stations easily despite the push and withdrawl of the surf. They remained as they were all that afternoon and were still in station the next day, giving us ample time to identify them through the glass as our first Brunnich's murres.

VIII

On September 14, 1492, less than a week after they had left the Canary Islands, "the crew of the Nina stated that they had seen . . . a tropic bird, or water-wagtail, which birds never go farther than twenty-five leagues from the land." Columbus, who played the role of ornithologist on his expedition before the science of ornithology had been inaugurated, lacked the scientific detachment of his successors. To him every bird was Noah's dove, heralding the appearance of land in the west. He had to keep up the courage of his crew in order to succeed in his mission, even at the expense of that truth which is an end in itself. When the log showed that they had already traveled a frightening distance without coming upon land, he falsified it to avoid panic and mutiny. When the compass-needles varied, he allayed their terror by telling them that the stars themselves had shifted position while the needles remained true. In the ignorance of their minds they must have believed that their Admiral knew the answer to every question, whereas what he did know implicity was the value of little lies in the achievement of great ends. So he told them that the tropic-bird was a sign of land when he was still almost a month's sailing from the first islands of the New World. But he, too, must have had his moments of panic, which he had to overcome in the solitude and darkness of his own mind, without the soothing advice of any superior officer who could claim a greater knowledge.

The first tropic-bird I ever saw appeared at sea in approximately the same latitude as the *Niña's,* though farther westward. It was late afternoon and the clouds were piled up in billowy masses from the horizon. Below, a rosy haze obscured their contours, but aloft, toward a blue sky, they stood out clear and white, their fullness modeled in light and shadow by the slanting rays of the sun. The bird appeared like a phantom against the confusing background, his sparkling whiteness picked out by one narrow sunbeam. He seemed to be engaged in some fantastic sky-dance as I first saw him, fixed in position while his wings flashed erratically. Suddenly he turned over, showing his whole silhouette with black-tipped wings and tail-feathers streaming upward, plunged toward the sea, and vanished in mid-air. The beam that had held him spot-lighted for an instant changed its form and dissolved. I could not find him again.

The next time I saw a tropic-bird was several years later, in the same waters, and this time he was not a phantom. He appeared close over the ship, flying with steady wing-beats like a pigeon, his yellow bill and streaming tail-feathers quite clear. He circled the steamer several times at the same leisurely pace, as his forefather may have circled the caravel *Niña,* and then made off to the horizon.

On September 16, Columbus came into the Sargasso Sea, where he comforted his crew by explaining the appearance of so much seaweed as a sure sign of land. On the eighteenth "Martin Alonzo in the Pinta which was a swift sailer, ran ahead of the other vessels, he having informed the Admiral that he had seen great flocks of birds towards the W. and that he expected that night to reach land." And from then on they came across birds nearly every day, though they were still in the center of the ocean. The next day two boobies came on board, and Columbus noted that "these birds are not accustomed to go twenty leagues from land." Also— "It drizzled without wind, which is a sure sign of land."

Undoubtedly Columbus had no eye for the æsthetic value of the birds he saw. The only occasions on which he allowed himself to enjoy the poetry of nature was when the weather reminded him of Andalusia in April, "wanting nothing but the melody of the nightingales," and that is easily understandable in a mariner who must have been as homesick as he was frightened, urging himself on by the demoniac power of his will against all the considerations of nature. Had those waters already been charted as they are now, he might have enjoyed the spectacle of the boobies with a more impartial mind, but he still would have been unable to say whether they were masked boobies, red-footed boobies, brown boobies, or gannets, since no Linnæus had yet arisen to make distinctions between species. In fact, he was so vague in applying names that one merely supposes the birds he mentions to have been boobies. One translator, no fol-

lower of Linnæus, gives them as pelicans, which is manifestly impossible since pelicans do not range over the open
ocean.

The birds probably appeared like flying crosses, with
long, slender white bodies and narrow wings tipped with
black. Since there was no wind, they beat swiftly over the
surface of the water, occasionally rising in broad arcs and
then plunging vertically, as they do today. But they had
never before seen the boats of the white men and their
curiosity evidently prompted them to alight for closer examination. They were not timid then, or are they now.

Toward night, on the twentieth, "two or three land
birds came to the ship, singing; they disappeared before
sunrise"—and right here one becomes suspicious that the
strain of the uncertainty was having its effect on the minds
of the observers. They were all overanxious for signs of
land, and they were still in the middle of an ocean that, as
far as they knew, had no end. It is possible that migrating
land birds might have been blown out to where the three
caravels sailed, but surely they would have been too exhausted to sing. On two different occasions, far from land,
swallows have spent the night aboard a ship in which I was
sailing, but in both cases they were so exhausted they could
be taken in the hand. A few feeble chirps was the nearest
they came to song. The song the journal mentions must
have been in the imaginations of the sailors exulting at the
sight of the visitors. For what encouragement they got came
chiefly from birds. Twice in that anxious month Columbus
is recorded as saying he misses only (that "only" was sheer
bravado) the song of the nightingale.

By October 7 the expedition was close enough to its goal
to be first witness to a migration of birds in the New World,

and it shifted its direction to conform to their course. "Towards evening . . . observing large flocks of birds coming from the N. and making for the SW., whereby it was rendered probable that they were either going to land to pass the night, or abandoning the countries of the North, he (the Admiral) determined to alter his course, knowing also that the Portuguese had discovered most of the islands they possessed by attending to the flight of birds." And all the night of October 9, two days before they sighted America, they heard birds passing.

In the same month of a year almost half a millennium after Columbus's first voyage I lay on the moonlit deck of a little boat in the Caribbean and listened to the cheeps and twitters of unseen land birds passing overheard in a steady stream on their way south.

This New World has aged in the centuries since Columbus sailed to discover it. The land has altered, and the people upon it, till it seems like immemorial time since the great Admiral wrote his journal. But the ever-changing sea he describes has remained unchanged. And when you read of the boobies and the tropic-birds and the man-o'-wars he saw in his passage, time no longer exists. For their wings are like the golden sandals of Athena described by Homer (himself an observer of the flight of sea birds three thousand years ago) that bore her always over the wet sea swift as the breath of the wind, and waxed not old.

A HAWK AT DUSK

A Hawk at Dusk

I T was as peaceful a scene as you might wish to see. The
month of May was still in that pristine stage when summer at last, after two months of false starts, begins to
come in like the tide at full flow. At this time of the year,
after winter has made its last stand in the gusts of April,
every day will mark a perceptible advance in the new season. Little jungles start up in the watered places; damp
rocks grow mossy; hard outlines become blurred. One
morning you awake to find that the weather-vane has veered
sharply to the south. All day a warm breeze that carries in
its seductive fragrance a new and voluptuous hope, a taste
of benefits to come, a promise of ease and bounty, washes
over the land; the horizon loses its corporeality, fades,
merges into a veil that softens all the lower reaches of the
sky. Nature, after six months of a clarity so inexorable that
it leaves no scope for the unknown, no refuge for illusion
within its emptiness, again becomes the fountainhead of
mysteries. Drama and passion return upon the stage, the
bare boards are covered in green, a veil is drawn over the
setting. And then the prelude begins with soft murmurs
that rise, spread, and swell out in chorus.

Within a few days the woods have grown immensely in
size. Where last week they were thin and transparent, exposing their limits to the casual gaze, your vision no longer
encompasses them. The breath of the tropics has brought

with it an obscurity within which the direct testimony of vision, confined as it is by fixed horizons, gives way to boundless imaginings. The border has become a misty and impenetrable barrier of green, the interior a vast gloom tenanted by moving lights and shadows, and by the originators of those countless rustling sounds that have no visible source. Yesterday you could see through its delicate fringe of green the structure of each individual tree. Bird songs could be traced to their source in the feathered bodies that shuttled between the twigs. Today the trees speak again with new voices, voices from the south, but you can find nothing. The lower limbs of the forest rise and spread into a mottled and confusing darkness in which the sight becomes lost. In the labyrinthine caverns strange rites are performed. Pan has returned. Elves scamper after him through dense underbrush that closes over their traces, leaving silence and dread. Others suddenly make a commotion overhead so that the whole roof of the forest shakes, but all you see is a yellow caterpillar dropping toward the ground on an invisible swinging thread. Then panic is near and it is better to escape again to the open.

In this season the Meadows are apt to turn green almost overnight. The Meadows are really all marsh, knee-deep in water, but from the hills in summer their true character is disguised by the thick swamp grass that rises above the surface. The hard white hummocks of straw that crackled underfoot yesterday are now lost in a sea of waving luxuriance. Birds and countless little beasts that are never seen by man have an inaccessible refuge here. They carry on their warfare and make their own peace on their own terms. In the early morning and again in the evening of these first warm days of May the Meadows ring with sound as if tiny bells were fastened to every rustling stalk of grass. The spring peepers sing in chorus from one end to the other, but you cannot find them out. Swamp sparrows call back and forth from hummock to hummock, marsh wrens chatter, yellow-throats lisp persistently. From deep in the alder jungles come thumps and watery gurgles and moaning sounds that have no explanation. You cannot investigate them, you cannot satisfy your curiosity by pursuit. This is no longer your world. Despite appearances, there is enough water overflowing its banks and streaming through the hummocks to drown a man.

You retreat over the hill with the skeletonesque windmill on top. The fan faces full south, revolving slowly. On such a day even the sky has become more expansive and friendly, the sky of the south that looks down indulgently on indolence. The malevolence of that gray pall through which the winter sun showed feebly, the turbulent and uncertain battleground of April across which heavy clouds maneuvered like a battle-fleet in action, give way before this warm stream of air from the south. The transition has been achieved, the enemy vanquished, peace enthroned. Hawks drift northward, high above, swallows swing low over the fields, reoccupying the country. The veil that obscures the far-off horizon has dissolved overhead, leaving a clear expanse of blue in which a few unformed cherubs float. Love has returned.

It is a perennial wonder how quickly and with what ease the country repairs the ravages of winter. Industry, handmaiden of peace, is immediately re-established in the wasted land. Cobwebs are spun in the trees, hornets ply between their hideouts and the surrounding neighborhood, bees tour through flower gardens and make special excursions to the wild blooms that have sprung up all over the fields. Artisans are busy with hive and nest. Courtship is carried on quite openly, with a total disregard of the secrecy that is to be expected in the frigid north. Peace, the beneficent, the sublime, the ineffable, reigns supreme in the land. She smiles down from the sky, she invests the breeze, she wards off evil.

In such times men should relax. Peace is abroad, to be savored only at leisure. Homage should be done her, pageants performed in her honor. A virgin decked out in flowers and flowing veils should tread a path of roses to the bridal chamber where she receives the mystic kiss of her lover. Epithalamiums should be chanted in chorus. Music and dancing in the fields should celebrate the harmony of love, and wine should be poured in tribute to her new fertility. Peace, in this recurring season, should find honor among men.

But the society of man knows no such seasonal respite. Peace must make headway in his ranks when she can, in season or out of season, for only the kingdom of nature is surely hers, and from that kingdom man has revolted. He has renounced the passive role of the receiver of gifts who offers in return only the ceremonial gratitude that is due to benevolence. He has explored better ways for a bounty that makes the ordinary gifts of nature seem paltry. By his own militant energy, by the sweat of his brow and the labor of his hands, he has found riches. But he has not found peace.

Now in early May when the skies are once more indulgent, when the earth is propagating life anew after the waste of winter, the newspapers are banners of war, full of hideous alarms and excursions, proclaiming imminent disaster and devastation. Great engines of mortality that they tell of are being primed for action, men march in step, with death seated in their hearts, whole populations tremble before the vision of an upraised fist. Terror spreads like smoke before the advancing flames, and diplomats plead with the representatives of the enemy for only one gesture to peace.

One gesture to peace! But peace is with you, all about you. There is no smoke in this sky. This great commotion that is made in the newspapers cannot change the fact that spring has come, that the sky shows a richer blue than for months past, that the earth is green and speaks with the industry of every insect and every bird in the land. We have seen these banners of war before, but we have seen no warfare. That is a matter of hysteria, of words on paper, of abstractions, ideas that occupy men's minds through the long winter. Which is real, the black marks left on white paper or the testimony of our senses? Which of these is truth? On such a day it seems unlikely that this season will hear the thunder of cannon, see the smoking fires of destruction. Not here, certainly, not now.

It was as peaceful a scene as you might wish to see. The day was drawing to a close. The sun had dropped below the tall hemlocks at the edge of the wood; but it still lighted up the weathercock that stood out over the cupola of the white barn, and the sky was radiant with the warm wash of evening light. The breeze from the south had died with the sunset, and the fan of the windmill that stood on the hill was motionless. From the roof of the little barn that abuts on the big one with the weathercock came a muffled cooing accompanied by the faint scraping of pigeon feet on boards. The pigeons who had been free all day had come into the loft to relieve their mates on the nests. They bowed and scuffled and pirouetted, puffing out their throats, uttering mournful rolling coos from deep in their pigeon interiors. The sound of their activity mingled with the evening sounds of the woods close at hand. A distant and continuous cawing of crows formed a background. Warblers chanted to each other through the massed foliage. And the whole scene was pervaded by that ubiquitous humming of nature in which no separate sound distinguishes itself, which seems to be rather an expression of the silence of space, the faint music of a sphere that rolls on oblivious to days and hours. The many voices were less piercingly urgent, they blended more gently into one another, each muted to the mood of the evening. Industry had come to an end—now leisure was the order of the hour. The serenity of a day well spent, of good works accomplished, of benefits received and destiny fulfilled, brooded over its finale. This was the hour when life relaxed a little, asking no more than passive acquiescence in the spectacle. Peace enfolded her own and waited for night to draw the curtain.

The pigeons were coming out of the loft for a last flight. They gathered along the ridgepole, emerging through the openings of the loft onto the narrow landings, blinking for a moment, then flapping up to the roof. The cocks drew in their heads, spread their tails against the shingles, let their heavy, iridescent throats hang slack, and rolled soft thunder about in their breasts. They pirouetted, they strutted after the hens, trod on their tails, followed them down to the eaves and up again. They danced and cooed and pecked at each other in passing. The hens held their heads high and walked delicately on the tips of their pink pigeon toes, as if shocked and put out by so much display of brute maleness. They were offended and a bit frightened. They flaunted their chastity, but were not above temptation. They were coy and elusive, side-stepping quickly away from their pir-ouetting mates. The loft was like a nunnery besieged by heroes.

Then one of them gave the panic signal. There was a sudden clatter of wings and the whole flock blew away as if a gigantic and invisible hand had swept them from the ridgepole. They swept down to the ground, wheeled all together, rose above the treetops, circled, and passed over our heads with a shrill whistling of wings. The sun came to life on the white underside of their pinions, spangling the air as they flashed past, all banking together for a turn. The second time they came aloft high up, so high that we could not be sure whether it was their wings we heard or a cat's-paw in the upper branches of the trees. The whole field passed high overhead, spread out, then massed together again, changing from black to white and back as the sun momentarily caught their wings. Then the lead bird col-lapsed, his wings went limp, he pitched headlong toward the ground as if shot. And after him the whole flock tum-bled, formation broken; every bird simultaneously went out of control. But, just in time, they all recovered, swept up into the sky again, and circled about the weathercock.

It was a spectacle of pure splendor and exultation. The birds flew, not in flight for their lives or in greedy pursuit, but merely because life was so strong in them that they could not stay quiet. They had to test their wings once more before they folded them for the night. They capered in high spirits, with pride in the strength and deftness of their pinions. One would suddenly cut loose from his mates, swing away from them, racing, snapping his wings like a whip; off into the sky in a great reverse circle, the stiff blades of his wings cutting deep; then in again, floating now, wings quivering like reeds as he settled once more into the bosom of the flock.

The pigeons were in a mood to play. They had mock stampedes when every bird would tumble as though a threat had appeared. It was great sport. Like a colt in pasture, close to the refuge of his mother's flanks, who shies and capers away from make-believe dangers, they dodged the attacks of an imaginary enemy from that sky that held in its warm and placid radiance only the serenity of perfect comfort and the untroubled security of peace.

Who can herald the approach of fear? No one sees it coming or hears the rustle of its footsteps in the leaves. Suddenly it is there, a gnawing, sinking sensation in the heart; not visible and palpable, to be grappled with, to be thrown down and overcome; merely a sickness of the nerves, a weakening of the will. It invades from within, paralyzing action and dissolving the cells of thought. It destroys the integrity of its victims and renders them incapable of organizing themselves for resistance. Unlike terror, which prompts action swifter than thought, it undoes the muscles and turns resolution to water so that its victims wait upon it helplessly.

No trumpet blasts announced the newcomer, no rolling tattoo of drums, no clash of cymbals. But, as if some strange and silent compulsion emanated from his presence, some attraction beyond resistance, our eyes fixed him instantly, fascinated by his slight form as he towered, unheralded, behind the barn. It was as if a fast pirate ship had suddenly appeared hull down on the horizon of a halcyon sea. With two flicks of his perfect wings the little falcon rose straight up out of the south, rose up on high to where he commanded the scene, a diminutive menace alone in that shining expanse. The sinking sun had gilded the sky like metal. In the east, dusk was already threatening. Against the rising gloom was a long thin stream of cloud as though a drop of oil had been wiped across a polished steel plate; and the horizon was somber. The pigeons had left off play, the spirit of freedom suddenly fallen from their wings, and were now circling in rapidly toward the barn, close above our heads. The rest of the sky was empty from end to end, except for the faint layer of cloud and the little falcon aloft in the south, a sable speck against its burnished brightness. The hemlock woods that banked against the barn on one side had darkened perceptibly, as if a shadow had fallen, and all of a sudden seemed tensely quiet. The warblers had for the moment hushed their chanting. The only sound was the intermittent rustling of the pigeons' wings as they circled overhead, drawing in close to the comfort of the loft. The serenity of the landscape had not been touched. There had been no disturbance of any sort, no reverberation of guns, no flash of lightning. Nothing distinguished the scene from what it had been a moment before except a mote against the sky, a little falcon no larger than a grain of dust.

Then the outlaw drew his narrow wings in close to his body and dropped obliquely across the sky toward the barn and the huddled flock circling over it. He was an exquisite and delicately shaped creature, smaller and finer in build than the birds whose company he was joining, with his slender body, long tail, and narrow pointed wings like gleaming knife-blades. As he drew near he spread his wings again and leveled out in his course, streaking past the weathercock. Now close behind the flock the wings were set in motion. They flicked sharply, each stroke like the snap of

a whip. The pigeons had massed together for security before their common danger, driven before the menace of a
pair of iron knuckles hidden in the approaching projectile.
Their wings flashed through the air in long downward
arcs, they stampeded out in a great racing circle over the
woods and back toward the barn with its fixed and indiffer-
ent weathercock. But the slender falcon was like fate in
flight, swifter and more powerful than mere pigeon mortality. He turned abruptly in full course, his wings almost
perpendicular to the ground, tail spread in a fan, and gained
a march on the flock. The gap was slowly lessening as the
field streaked overhead again. Now you could see every
detail of the predator's jewel-like perfection, the slaty blue
wings, the tail barred with white, the darkly streaked underparts. His form was superb. He banked sharply for every
turn, pinions and tail spread wide, with no diminution of
his ruthless pace, and each time drew closer to the racing
pigeons. In the straightaway he was like a deadly piece of
precision machinery working at high speed, his long stiff
pinions whipping the air as he closed in for the kill.

Suddenly there was real terror. The last pigeon of the
flock went off at an hysterical tangent with winged horror
only a few lengths from his tail. He veered in panic toward
a grove of elms growing in the open, hurtled toward them
in a long descending arc, turned and twisted among their
trunks, and as the threat descended on him plunged headlong onto the ground. The pigeon rebounded once and
rolled over at the base of the trees, momentarily stunned
by his fall. But the falcon threw up sharply, swung out in a
wide racing curve, and returned after the flock.

The pigeons were still circling about the weathercock.
If you had not seen the hawk, or had mistaken him

for another pigeon (as well you might without observing closely), you would have found this flight of doves part of a peaceful twilight scene, appropriate to the close of a day of rare loveliness, of gentle placidity. The air was soft, balmy, and fragrant. The evening light was conducive to dreaminess, and the soft rustling of the pigeons' wings as they passed overhead lulled one with a sense of infinite peace and security. In the distance a tree-toad, anticipating the night, was calling in a gentle tremolo. Even a wood-thrush was now singing his vespers from deep in the woods, his easy, sonorous tones, interspersed with trills and grace notes, voicing the melancholy and repose of a world that was ready for sleep.

The little falcon was once more close upon the flock. The sleek pigeons with their iridescent throats swept in terror overhead like a band of winged projectiles, the air whistling through their pinions. They circled out over the woods in close formation, all acting in unison, responding to one impulse. The falcon, more delicately constructed for his deadly mission, brought up the rear.

He was following one bird now, pursuing it as one pigeon pursues another in courtship flight, responding to every maneuver of its attempt at escape. Slowly he closed in, and as the flock streaked overhead he seemed finally to merge with the bird of his choice. At the same instant there was a puff of white in the air, like smoke from the guns of a man-of-war. But one waited in vain for the thunder that should have followed. The downy feathers drifted to the ground after the flock had passed on, descending as gently through the stillness as if an angel in heaven had merely dusted them from his wings.

The pigeons had taken a long turn about the windmill,

death with them, flying in their midst like a member of the fold in good standing. Once about the windmill and then they came back, wheeling over the woods. Again a victim was marked out, detached from the others, and pursued. The pigeon lost his head, like a dog with a can tied to his tail, and fled wildly toward the loft that embodied all the comfort he knew. The horror was just above and behind him, in a position to strike with the hard knuckles of his talons. Only a desperate maneuver could save him now. Then the little falcon turned over and stooped on the bird, which plunged in panic toward the wide roof of the barn. Both birds had their wings set in close to their bodies. They dove steeply and streaked low over our heads, the air screaming through their stiff pinions in a long wail that ended with a hollow, sickening thud as the pigeon, unable to save himself, struck the roof with all the force of his plunge. The hawk, his wings and tail quickly braced, threw up high in the air over the barn and circled back, while the pigeon rolled heavily down the slope of the roof and fell stunned to the ground.

Dusk had spread up from the horizon in the east and was now absorbing the last light of day like a sheet of gray blotting paper. The earth, the windmill on the hill, the stolid weathercock, and the hemlock trees alongside the barn were losing their solidity and darkening against the sky. From the woods a warbler, insensible to the drama of the scene, shot up above the treetops singing wildly, as if lifted on a fountain of song, then dropped back silent into the forest. There were one or two scattered caws from the crows in the distance, followed by quiet.

The pigeons were still circling over the barn, their wings rustling like silk each time they passed overhead. But now that night was so close, the pirate seemed to have given up the pursuit. For the first time since he had appeared he slackened his pace. He circled once toward the flock, changed his mind, and took a new course. Now he rose up above the windmill and circled with pinions outspread and motionless; then drew them in to his body and dropped obliquely out of the sky toward the Meadows on the other side of the hill. The pigeons passed overhead, dropping lower now, the whole flock quivering. Then, with one accord, they all braced themselves with wing and tail, flapped heavily, and dropped down onto the ridgepole. They stood there, motionless and weary, savoring the returning peacefulness of descending night. The tree-toads were singing in chorus, calling and answering on every side. A garden toad from behind the barn let out a soft moan that was suddenly quenched. A gray pall of slumber seemed to have descended on the scene, and after a few moments of uncertainty the night sounds of early May were coming into their own. The pigeons stood quietly on the ridgepole, their heads high, their little eyes alert; but already forgetfulness was on the way, their little memories were growing dim. With the disappearance of the hawk recollection of panic faded. Fear weakened, uncoiled, and finally slid away altogether. Now peace the enchantress, peace who pities us all, returned to the flock.

Nothing had happened—nothing at all. The pageant of life resumed where it had been broken off. Cock pigeons danced again in the magic light of evening before demure and hesitating mates. They spread their tails against the shingles, ruffled all their feathers, puffed out their heavy throats for the soft utterance of their passion. The hens made a great display of chastity, but were obviously not beyond temptation. They drew out their necks, held their heads high, and with glittering eyes looked as alarmed as they possibly could. They edged delicately away from the pirouetting cocks, with coy mincing steps of their little pigeon feet, and pretended to be dreadfully shocked by the vulgar, the unmistakable advances of their mates.

From beyond the hill a whip-poor-will called now, signaling the approach of night. A star glittered dimly in the east. The pigeons, one or two at a time, walked down to the eaves, dropped to the narrow landings below, and went inside. Sleep was coming to banish the cares of daylight, to soothe wounded spirits, to restore a world that had fulfilled with honor the mission of its day. Soon an owl hooted twice from far away in the woods. The reverberation of his soft war-call passed over the silent Meadows, crossed the hills, penetrated faintly into the barnyard.

But the pigeons knew nothing of the night. They were secure in their sanctuary, roosting on the firm rafters, their heads tucked blissfully into the oblivious darkness of their wings. . . . All except one, who remained on the ground under the eaves of the barn. Now that the horror had passed away he had found his feet again. He stood there, silent, dazed, and motionless, in a world of growing darkness.

THE LITTLE TYRANT

The Little Tyrant

IN birds as in men, if it's valor you want you had better look among the smaller sizes. Only the small fully realize the meaning of that word. Your Goliaths may have stout enough hearts, but they can never match the Davids of this world in shows of valor; their size is against them. Little Napoleon, with his white belly, his blue coat, and his cocked hat not much above five feet from the ground, may have had many hulking corporals in his guard, but surely none so valorous as he.

And now that I think of it, the little kingbird bears a quite noticeable resemblance to the little corporal. Outwardly, of course, the similarity is unmistakable. There is the same white belly contrasting with a dark coat, the disproportionately large head with its red cockade. Napoleon ruled the eagles of France, of Austria, of Germany, and almost (if winter had only delayed) of Russia; similarly the kingbird, whose official Latin title, *Tyrannus tyrannus*, you might interpret as Tyrant of Tyrants, dominates all eagles and lesser hawks that have the temerity to approach his kingdom. During the warm months there is no doubt in these parts of who rules. Only winter can accomplish his overthrow and drive him into exile. And that is easily understandable, for the kingbird is really a foreigner here, speaking with a strange Latin accent, hailing from warmer southern climes. Almost all of the 358 members of his family live exclusively in the tropics.

Considering what a dominant figure the kingbird was in our political economy this past summer, his arrival was singularly unobtrusive. Nothing like the blackbirds' display of force distinguished it. He did not marshal his strength in the sky, or utter trumpet-calls to give notice of his advent. Merely—one morning at the beginning of May —there he was, white belly gleaming, massive black head planted squarely on stalwart shoulders, sitting on a telephone wire that gave him command of a grassy field in which flying insects that ventured too close were singled out for annihilation and promptly dispatched. He was clearly a soldier of merit, but as yet he showed none of those domineering traits that later won him unquestioned supremacy. There were other good soldiers in the field too. A bluebird, perched a foot or two away on the wire, was accepted as his equal. A sparrow hawk, hovering out over the middle of the field, went unchallenged. But when he performed his maneuvers, no doubt remained about the kingbird's dominant character, should he ever choose to exercise it.

A foolish winged insect, thinking nothing of the stalwart bird so far below him, throws his insignificant shadow on that alert eye and in the same instant the kingbird is off, rising straight up with a rapid flutter of wings. Before the victim has time for more than one vain dodge, that broad bill has snapped up his life, and the conqueror, his pointed wings now rigid, his tail spread in a white-bordered fan, is falling through the air to land with a little flourish on the exact spot that he has just vacated. A series of snaps of his bill, sounding like castanets accidentally rattled, and the insect has vanished from the sunshine that gave it life. With the kingbird it is all one, two, three. The bluebird is not remotely in the same class. He waits until he sees a crippled moth fluttering lamely in the grass below and falls down to capture it finally after a wrestling-match in which it seems, for a moment, as if the moth is going to get the better of his assailant. When the bluebird has finally made his meal he must pause in the grass to recover before he again climbs up to his lookout. The sparrow hawk is as neat as the king-bird in his maneuvers, but he, too, habitually looks down for his prey.

After that first meeting I did not see the kingbird for several days. As usual, there was no migrational abundance of kingbirds in our region, no passage of battalions pausing for a day or two on their way north. Though the little tyrant is a common summer resident over most of the North American continent, he manages, like the other flycatchers, to come and go without attracting attention. He is here, he is gone; but the actual passage, the process by which he translates himself from Bolivia to British Columbia, from Peru to Quebec, from Panama to New York, I have almost never seen.

And that is all the more strange because no other bird is so open in his dealings, so unreserved in the revelation of his private life. He fears no one and hides nothing. Whether he is building a house or courting his queen, he makes himself as conspicuous as possible, scorning to adopt the timid methods of the lesser birds that hide behind shrubbery and dart to cover at the squeak of a mouse. No, his defense against the universe, and the universe might as well know it, is attack, ruthless, swift, and open. Let others hide from him; he carries on in full view, exposing his black and white uniform against the sky as a challenge to all challengers.

He does not fly by night, like so many of the weaker birds; neither does he require the security of large flocks. I assume that his migration must be of a more casual sort in our parts, that he moves from tree to tree, from fence to post, hawking for insects as he goes, and so journeys northward without giving any hint of the fact that he is engaged in the arduous biannual duty of migration.

The obscure, unreasoned impulse which had carried the kingbird across thousands of miles of trackless jungle and open sea first became manifest toward the end of May, when he and his newly acquired mate, who had flown north on the same mission, began to take an uncommon interest in a small, skimpy, neatly pruned apple tree that grows near the house. Quite simply they proclaimed their ownership. They guarded that tree as though it bore the golden apples of the Hesperides, towering together over it on quivering wings, reiterating constantly their high, rolling war-call. All day long there were excursions back and forth to the tree, meetings of both kingbirds accompanied by shrieking welcomes and exhibitions of hovering, darting, swooping, and stationary flight. It seemed as if nature had filled these thimbles with an inexhaustible ocean of vitality.

In a few days the goal of this tireless activity began to take shape in the form of a bundle of dried grass and weeds loosely tied to a couple of twigs at one of the outermost extremities of the apple tree. The fact that the nest was badly tilted worried me for the next month. I should have liked to offer some helpful criticism of its architecture. But it was all right, the kingbirds knew what they were doing.

When the building itself had been completed, such as it was, they set about the fussier task of interior decoration, hunting out bits of thistledown and dandelion for warmth and comfort. This meant abandoning their celestial habitat and condescending to visit the ground occasionally, down among the robins and the sparrows. But, aerial beings that they were, they did not have the proper shape for posing on lawns. Their little feet did not lift them high enough, their habitually erect posture flattened their tails against the ground. With their gleaming white shirt-fronts and black coats they looked, from the front view, for all the world like miniature penguins that had suddenly found themselves on a green carpet and did not quite know what to do about it. And it never occurred to them that feet could be used for locomotion; they fluttered their wings even for the conquest of inches.

In most forms of animal life the propagation of the race seems to be a purely unintentional outcome of the sexual impulse, which is directed toward the satisfaction of the moment rather than the population of the future. A physical need exists to be satisfied, and its satisfaction involves remote consequences which were certainly not considered at the moment. Among birds, however, procreation is not the incidental consequence of an impulsive act, but the end of a chain of action that seems to have been deliberately followed with the sole purpose of bringing into being a new generation. There is no trace of capriciousness in the history of their mating. The ruling impulse seems to be the production of a family, and the physical union merely one of several incidental means to that premeditated end. They put as much passion into the choice of a nesting site, the building of the nest, the brooding of the eggs, and the feeding of the young, as into the act of union itself. The male lavishes as much devotion and protecting care on his nest as on his mate, and fights as readily in its defense.

Still, I don't for a moment suppose that birds, who are creatures of impulse and incapable of contemplation, can visualize the remote future consequences of their acts. We must not allow the lower forms of life credit for spiritual faculties that even we possess imperfectly. The kingbird, leading the abundant life somewhere in the jungles of tropical America, was not suddenly overcome last spring by the appalling thought that if he and his mates did not act promptly his species might disappear from the earth. He did not think of Duty. He did not think of a nest and a clutch of fertile eggs, of embryonic life stirring, or fledglings trying out their fledgling wings over a neat green lawn some thousands of miles distant. He did not think at all. Nevertheless, he was possessed by an urge, some obscure, unrealized impulse, some restlessness which made him less content to stay where he was, even though there had been no change in his outward circumstances. The jungle still offered the same abundant food and shelter. The sun still shone, flowers bloomed, insects hummed, night and day alternated as usual. Nevertheless, the periodic urge, which scientists have guessed arises from seasonal glandular changes in the body's interior, was there. I suppose it may have been several weeks before it was strong enough to prompt action. However that may be, the time came when he found himself flying northward to alleviate the urgency which he did not understand. It was merely that he felt better about flying north than about flying east or west or south, or remaining where he was. Surely he did not picture that neatly pruned apple tree on the lawn outside our house, even though he may have nested in its immediate vicinity less than a year earlier. I doubt that at any point he saw beyond his actual physical horizon. He embarked on a journey that must have fazed him had he been capable of grasping its magnitude. A man would have to be endowed with exceptional courage to undertake it. But courage is needed only where there is imagination, and the kingbird had no need of it.

I have seen something of the lands through which my kingbird passed on his way to our plot of ground, and to me his journey has a glamour that he could never comprehend. He traveled through countries with exotic names like Ecuador, like Guatemala, as a man passes Fifth Street and Fourth Street every morning on his way to the office. He had no appreciation of names and their meaning, of social or historical geography. The monumental stone ruins of ancient civilizations hidden in the forests were on a par with our frame garage near the apple tree. The clumps of palms slanting out over turbid alligator rivers, the spreading ceiba trees standing before white plaster churches in remote Indian villages, the breadfruit trees with their strangely patterned leaves, the giant mahoganies in which he perched, were no different from our poplars. Smoldering volcanoes meant nothing. I have seen the kingbird in these tropical lands—possibly the very kingbird—but I have seen no gleam of romance in his eye. He was hawking after insects in the same business-like manner there as here. An insect is an insect, a tree is a tree, earth is earth, sky sky. What have latitude and longitude to do with that?

Nevertheless, I like to think of that passage as a Great Adventure. It is a purely human weakness. I must attach my proper interpretation to an improperly vicarious experience. In my mind it remains the Great Adventure to which my kingbird was summoned by Destiny, by the Fate of his species. Hardly larger than a golf-ball, with a black tailcoat, pointed wings, a head punctuated by two soberly alert black eyes, that little kingbird flew over green oceans of tropical forest, with monkeys sunning themselves in the branches below, spotted jaguars creeping along dark limbs, macaws screaming and displaying their brilliant plumage against the rank foliage—and all in order that the great mission of racial survival might be accomplished in that skimpy apple tree on the lawn.

The Bird of Destiny was ambitious, but never with his own ambition. Always that same obscure urge directed his strength. He flew through high valleys encircled by volcanic mountains. He crossed long stretches of land in which the only vegetation was thorn-bush and cactus, where giant lizards stood motionless against the brown sand. He saw countless rugged gorges through which torrents of muddy water poured from the mountains into the sea. The urge, which never left him, was strongest in the morning, after he had fed. But sometimes it may have been stronger even than his appetite, and then he went to roost with an empty crop. Again, he flew northward all night because there was nothing but ocean below. When the coastline he was following curved back from the north he unhesitatingly took out across the open sea, knowing (and at the same time not knowing) that there was land beyond. The impulse to leave the coast was informed by intelligence, but by an intelligence that was not his own. Beyond the ocean he came across another land, a land of parks and gardens, of cultivated fields and patches of woodland, of busy villages and towns. And at the end of the journey stood the beacon of Destiny, the goal of the Great Adventure, that little apple tree on the lawn between our house and the garage.

Not, however, the final goal, the ultimate haven of rest for the weary; the urge that had carried him across land and sea did not leave him when he arrived. But he stopped here now because it no longer satisfied that urge to go farther. Still obedient to his fate, he claimed the apple tree as his stage and waited, knowing (and not knowing) that the solitary first labor of his mission had been accomplished, that from now on he would have a mate to share his duties. And sure enough, within a few days he was joined at his post by another kingbird, who took for granted his presence and his inclinations as he took for granted her arrival. With the apple tree as their chosen setting they played their traditional parts to a single rhythm, for both wills were bent by the same motive, prompted by the same series of momentary inspirations, subject to the same transcending intelligence that both followed blindly.

It is easy enough to conjure up the picture of a pleasant domestic scene to describe the family life of the kingbird—something on the order of the hearth-loving English vicar of the nineteenth century, surrounded by devoted wife, clay pipe, and three affectionate daughters. The early flutterings of mutual love in the respective breasts, the ripening of a maturer affection as family cares impose sobriety—protective affection in the male, devoted and worshipful in his mate. . . . The thing has been done. It was quite the fashion some years ago to draw moral sustenance from the examples of the good life set us by our feathered brethren. This was done chiefly, I believe, by ladies, closet ornithologists who rarely ventured out of sight of their pet canaries, though the literary clergy may also have had a hand in it. But the age of moral elevation has passed, and the feathered brethren, like the unfeathered, have had their manners corrupted by the literature of an irresponsible new age. Times change, birds change.

Take, for example, the matter of Candide and Cune-gonde, a pair of pearl-gray diamond doves I kept in a cage some years back. A gentler, more refined couple, judging from appearance, I never had the happiness of knowing. There was no doubt, when you looked at them, that Candide combined good sense with *"l'esprit le plus simple,"* or that Cunegonde was a worthy match for him in every way. He had the good manners and the air of naïve idealism, of mild elegance together with rare purity of soul, that might have characterized a simple country gallant of the eighteenth century whose chief joy was to woo the maiden of his choice in those *fêtes champêtres* that recaptured the felicity of shepherds in Arcady. He seemed wrought from mother-of-pearl rather than the coarse clay that went into our own flesh. When he was courting Cunegonde one could almost hear the music of the minuet. The courtship always began at a respectful distance from the object of his worship. Usu-ally she was on a perch near the top of the cage and he on the floor at her feet. He would bow low before her, spread-ing his long, pointed tail in a fan over his head, and simul-taneously utter sounds so soft, so plaintive and appealing, that they must have melted the heart of an eagle had any been near. The very air seemed to swoon with their softness. But Cunegonde was too bashful to be won so easily. You could see that she was flattered, you could almost sense the quickening of her pulse. But she would remain coy and aloof, pretending not to notice or to be in the least affected by the ceremonious courtship of her lover. Gradually the rhythm of the bows and tail-spreadings, with their accom-panying cooings, would grow more marked, would take on a dramatic throbbing character, till finally they had become the chief figures in a sort of dance in which he wove backward and forward on the delicate tips of his little pink feet. Still Cunegonde would be coy. Candide would interrupt his courtship once or twice to stare at her from one side of his head, as if wondering whether it might not be a stuffed bird that he was wasting his attentions on, and each time resume his dance with redoubled intensity, as much as to say that even the dead could be brought to life, if such were the case. Soon there could no longer be any doubt that passion had crept into the performance. But worse would follow. Beside himself with exasperation, finally, Candide would leap with a flash of wings to the perch beside Cunegonde, and, forgetting his manners altogether . . .

I cannot conscientiously report that my kingbirds underwent any mystical or moral experience in the process of their union. As far as I could tell it was a purely practical matter. One after another, the female produced four eggs in the interior of her body, and one after another her mate fertilized them, acting exactly as though he had a perfect understanding of the mysterious processes of egg-production and embryogeny. His advances and her acceptances were spaced, as though by intelligence, to fit into the established rhythm of procreation. When, for the first time, she began to spend the night in their nest while he went off alone to roost in the woods, I knew that the spotted eggs had already been deposited in the pocket especially built to contain them.

The kingbird's days of freedom were definitely over. One may assume that his liberty had already been severely qualified ever since that urge which he had first felt in distant lands had taken possession of him. "Free as a bird" is an expression in which a bird might find ironical amusement; especially as coming from man, the only animal who has, in his individual life, succeeded in achieving some measure of independence from the discipline of nature. But now the kingbird's responsibility was embodied in four small white spheroids spotted with umber. He had a concrete treasure to guard. Those fragile shells contained the future of his race, the reason for his long migration, the cause to which he had been dedicated many weeks earlier and thousands of miles away. It was no longer enough to guard his own person from enemies. At last he had a treasure, a treasure which lay in an open nest exposed to enemies who would ravish it at the first relaxation of the vigil he shared with his mate.

Crows, especially, were dangerous. By inherited instinct, if not by experience, the kingbird knew that they would eat his eggs and young if he allowed them occasion, and, following the Napoleonic policy of his species that the best form of defense is an effective offense, he never gave the crows a chance to launch an attack. I don't suppose it was really policy. Again, he seemed prompted by a racial intelligence that was not his own. Whenever a crow appeared on the distant horizon, though he were only passing peacefully by and minding his own business, the kingbird and his mate, with piercing shrieks of anger, would project themselves at him like a pair of missiles shot out of the tree by the force of their own energy. It was unreasonable, but effective. Darting at him from above, and occasionally landing on his back in mid-flight, they would soon have him plunging like a maddened horse under a swarm of bees, and it was a pretty sure thing that he would make a long detour the next time his business carried him that way. Unreasonable, but extremely effective. The piratical crows were the first to be driven out of our neighborhood when the kingbirds set about establishing their kingdom.

In those early days, however, before the embryos had developed in the eggs, it was enough to guard them from nest-robbers. The constant brooding, to insure the proper temperature for their development, came later. The kingbirds were still free to expend their limitless vitality in exhibition flights, hawking for insects and harassing the neighborhood birds. Occasionally one or the other of them would rest for a while on the eggs, but any excuse to abandon them was good enough.

You might have thought that both birds were expert embryologists from the way they seemed to know just how much brooding was necessary, increasing the amount gradually from day to day. But they had read no book on the prenatal care of birds, attended no course of lectures, studied no diagrams. They did not know the contents of those eggs or the purpose of their brooding. They did not know why they had produced them, or why they had ever built a nest to contain them; or why they now bothered to guard them. Nor could previous experience, rule of thumb acquired through trial and error, have been a basis for their actions, since birds will follow the same established procedure whether or not they are nesting for the first time. I rather think it was the lack of any intelligent comprehension of their own actions that made those actions possible. Calculation would merely have confused the process. Completely devoid, as they were, of the capacity for reasoning, for weighing alternatives, for valuing ends, their natural instincts, shaped over millennia of evolution to the sole end of survival, had no rivalry to their leadership, authority was undivided. They acted blindly because their actions were only reflections of intuition; they acted surely, without hesitation, because only intuition prompted their actions.

The perfect co-operation between the two prospective parents was another indication of the integrity of instinct they shared in common. When the female had brooded long enough and was ready to leave the nest in search of food or exercise, she did not call her mate into consultation and ask him to take her place. She merely followed her urge and departed. The male would sometimes delay for several minutes after her departure, but you could see that the empty nest concerned him. When the safe time had elapsed, he would fly over and settle down in her place, folding his wings carefully for a long vigil. Gradually the time between watches was reduced, as the developing embryos required more constant warmth, until in the last stages the birds would replace each other immediately.

It will be no surprise to the reader who has followed the history of the kingbirds this far to learn that their eggs did finally split open and bring forth the renewed life of the species in the form of four pink dabs of flesh, with eye-slits for eyes, with ludicrously disproportionate bills and feet, and with wing-stumps that were far from having the aerodynamic perfection of the adults' feathered pinions. And yet, how can it be otherwise than surprising? Here was an achievement out of all proportion to the kingbirds' limited powers; the culminating fourth act of a drama played over two continents, involving the most sweeping action and the most subtle dialogue, by two insignificant actors whose limited powers, placed at the disposal of the unlimited forces of nature, had produced this immortality. By themselves, these two little birds had no powers of generation. They lacked the intelligence and the knowledge to understand the necessary processes. The two kingbirds who had performed this exploit were but the instruments of an inscrutable and disembodied will, a universal purpose heard only in the echo of their own unpondered desires.

The kingbirds themselves were not surprised when they felt the eggs stirring beneath them. As passive instruments of an unfathomable fate they accepted as they performed, without fear or question. And now the labor of the performance was increased by the necessity of filling those four bottomless gullets. Time was passing. Summer was half gone. Quantities of young robins, bluebirds, phoebes, had taken possession of the countryside and were already feeding themselves. Insects were plentiful. The kingbirds perched on the topmost twigs of the trees adjacent to their nest-tree and every minute or two sallied forth to bring in some new prey. At midday, when the sun beat down with tropical intensity, one or the other of them would stand guard on the edge of the nest, wings spread to shelter the unfeathered young from its rays. In the evening, as the heat began to wear off, the young would grow increasingly clamorous, and both parents would be hard pressed to keep them satisfied with tributes of insects until nightfall.

Up to now the kingbirds had paid little attention to me, evidently not classing my kind with such worthy opponents as crows and hawks. Along with rabbits, muskrats, groundhogs, and white-footed mice, I was considered harmless. They did not even flatter me by trying to hide their nest or dissemble their concern for it in my presence. All other birds I have been familiar with have at least had some hesitation about approaching their nests (always hidden) when I was observing them. But that was never a kingbird's way. Like the stalwart fighter he is, he has no need of trickery or deception. He builds his nest and rears his young in full view; let anyone approach at his peril. Only when I took

advantage of their openness to get some photographs of
them did the kingbirds change their estimate of me. That
machine I carried raised me definitely to the status of a
menace. From that moment I could call the crows my equals.
Hovering overhead with shrill staccato shrieks, they took
turns in plunging at me, their flaming crests, never displayed
except in battle, standing erect on their heads, their bills
snapping like the strokes of doom. So fierce was the onslaught that, despite my manifest advantages, I felt something of the terror that must accompany the insect's instant
of annihilation. The first plunge brought me to my knees,
my arms clasping my head for protection. But they could
not drive me away. Eventually the clamor of the young for
food forced them to abandon the attack, and I got the
photographs I wanted. After that, however, I was a marked
man. Camera or no camera, whenever I entered their territory (which was anywhere up to a hundred yards from the
tree) they charged me. Other men could come and go as they
pleased; I had earned their undying enmity by my invasion
of their privacy. They knew now that I, different in that
from others of my kind, had taken an interest in their nest
and young, and they could not know that my interest was
benevolent.

Of course they were right not to take any chance. They
were eminently right in everything they did; as witness the
fact that the four dabs of flesh grew rapidly in a few days'
time to fully fledged reproductions of their elders, and were
soon out of the nest. No ceremony accompanied their departure, no ostentation. In fact, it was anything but deliberate. The young birds were literally pushed out into the
world by their own growth. They hatched from the nest as
they had hatched from those spotted eggs, only when it

could no longer contain them. Their reluctance was marked. The first day they merely tried their footing on the edge of the nest and along the adjacent twigs; and by evening all had crowded back into the cradle. One can understand their unwillingness to say farewell to the day of their infancy. But time does not wait on the pleasure of mortals. The next night the four kingbirds roosted all in a row beside an abandoned nest, and in the morning they embarked on their first experimental flights, fluttering across the great open spaces between twig and twig.

I cannot say the parent birds took any pride in the achievement. From first to last their attitude was strictly business-like. They maintained the food-supply and kept all enemies at a distance, but I never saw them give their progeny any sign of encouragement or commendation in those first attempts to cope with the problem of flight. The young birds now had to take their share of the responsibility for their own survival. When one of them, weaker and less developed than the others, with a mere stump of tail and inadequate pinions, fell out of the tree in an abortive attempt at flight, he was left to lie where he fell, exposed to all the dangers that creep on the ground. Had it not been for my benevolent intervention, which made me the target of a series of breath-taking attacks, he would never have escaped the universal fate of weaklings. Again the kingbirds were right. According to the strictly practical ethics of nature, the Spartan code which subordinates the individual to the race, the weak must always die so that the strong may survive. But, mere man that I was, a renegade from nature and the child of a decadent humanitarian age, I followed the less practical ethics of my kind, which assume that the kingdom of nature is governed by a Bill of Rights based on the political philoso-

phy of the eighteenth century, assuring, in the mystic name
of Justice, the participation of weak and strong alike in the
goods of this earth. My fault was human. But the kingbirds
were right. The next day that same fledgling fell out of the
tree again, and again I replaced him, in the teeth of their
violent opposition. I don't suppose he survived the year,
however. There are too many pitfalls in the path and only
the strong and warlike can hope to hold their place on the
program of nature.

I have heard a good many stories about the fierceness of a
lioness in the defense of her cubs, but I would set my kingbird up against any lioness, real or legendary. Now that the
young were out in the open, exposed to the attack of every
passing hawk, he and his mate were transformed into a pair
of Furies who anticipated the need of vengeance by harry-
ing the countryside with a fierce, demoniac rage. The
smaller birds were unmolested as long as they kept their distance. But an interdict was issued against all greater fowl,
especially the hawks, who were proscribed from showing
themselves anywhere within the circle of the horizon. No
longer was there peace in the land. At any moment the air
might be torn by the staccato shrieks of the kingbirds and I
would spin about in time to see them go sizzling into the
sky like a pair of rockets after a distant speck of a hawk
passing through on the way to his feeding grounds. They
always attacked from above, and the harassed hawk never
made any attempt to meet the challenge except by escape.

I must not give the impression that the kingbirds were
prompted to assault an enemy so much more powerful than
themselves by mere recklessness. As children of nature they
were far too practical for that. Napoleon may have been a
romanticist in his aims, but he was an utter realist in policy;

until the end he never attacked except with a realistic confidence in his own superiority. The kingbird, similarly, knew his own powers and the strength of the enemy, and he reckoned accordingly. Note that he always attacked from above, the one position in which he was safe from retaliation. For no large bird, however much advantage it may have in speed or sustained flight, can climb as rapidly as a small bird. The small birds have not the weight necessary for high speed or for gliding flight, but for the same reason they are more buoyant, more easily raised by the strokes of their wings. Often too easily. Most of the small birds must fold their wings and drop down at regular intervals to maintain a level course. The typical rising and falling flight of the perching birds is directly due to this excess buoyancy. The kingbird's manner is different. He is exceptional in the control he can exercise over his speed and pitch by varying the depth of his wing-strokes rather than their frequency. But the same buoyancy is his. I have seen my kingbird ascend almost vertically for twenty or thirty feet to capture some insect passing overhead. A hawk cannot make so steep a grade. His method is to rise slowly in sweeping circles till he has reached his pitch, and from there to prey on what lies below him. The kingbird knew that he was safe in his attack as long as he remained above. Even so, he never quite closed in, as he did with crows, being careful always to keep a few inches' leeway between himself and the hawk he was storming. His tactics were always shrewd, rather than reckless.

I mention the kingbird's realism in this respect with no derogation to his valor. He had no more use for romanticism in making war than in making love. With confidence in his own powers, he used them fully, but he reflected the

will of nature too exactly to be other than strictly practical
in his policy. As with all great rulers, his sovereignty was a
masterly achievement of *Realpolitik*. There was no nonsense in his make-up.

I am not much given to hero-worship, but before the
summer was over I was persuaded that the kingbird could
do no wrong. To a human being, endowed with the intelligence and imagination that distract men from their purpose, confuse their policy, and lead them into a morass of
doubts and hesitations, the kingbird's ever-unhesitating
choice of the right course could only command admiration.
He never wavered between alternatives. He never ques-
tioned. He was never uncertain. And he was always amaz-
ingly right. The triumph of his sovereignty was inevitable
from the first because it was inevitable that he should always
use his powers to their best advantage. In the strength of his
single-mindedness that little mite, not so big as my fist, became a symbol of invincible purpose in nature.

The kingdom which he had come up from the south to
establish in our apple tree was now justified by four brand-
new princes clothed in the traditional black-and-white of
their kind, their breasts immaculate, their tails tipped with
white, the feathers of wing and back still fresh and unworn.
It had taken them only a few days to learn proper kingbird
flight, and now they knew all the tricks: how merely to vi-
brate their wing-tips for hovering and how to dig deep in
the sprints, how to spread their tails for sudden turns, how
to change their pace without interval, and how to glide in
to their landings on motionless pinions. They accompanied
their parents about the countryside in a screaming procession and flew after them to snatch prey from their bills in
mid-air. Only the fact that their plumage was now shabby,

that their breasts had darkened and the white edges of their wing-feathers worn off, distinguished the parents from their offspring. But the moulting season was at hand, and when the six kingbirds took their separate departures for the tropics there would no longer be any way of telling them apart.

Simultaneously with the development of the young birds' capacity to care for themselves, the inscrutable urge which had driven the kingbird over thousands of miles of land and sea, had prompted him to build a nest and take a mate, and had aroused in him a concern for the fledglings that resulted from the union, lost its strength. When the young birds no longer depended on him they became strangers and possible rivals who might, when the next nesting season came round, be attacked with as much vigor as they had been cherished during their upbringing. His mate became merely another bird whose existence did not concern him. Once more he was free of ties and responsibility.

Almost free, but not quite. As long as mortal beings are subject to the passage of time, the constant revolution of the four seasons, the steady march of days and hours—each minute leaving its faint, ineffaceable mark so that there can be no turning back from the universal end—as long as the earth and all its inhabitants continue to grow older, they can never be quite free. The kingbird's mission had been successfully accomplished, another generation had been produced. But there was some loss: a whole season of life had passed away. In a few more weeks the insects on which he depended for his livelihood would be gone, the leaves would be stripped from the trees, the first wintry frosts would wither the verdure of summer. Again he must move.

With millions of other birds, the majority pursuing their

first migration (he no longer recognized his offspring among them), he began to drift southward. He had no vision of the approach of winter, for he could never have experienced it. But now a new urge had taken possession of him, growing stronger with the weeks. His life was once more shaped to a deliberate will which commanded it. That southern course was not new to him, but time had passed since he had last flown it, another year had been taken from the term of his life.

I like to picture my kingbird arriving once more in tropical lands on a warm November evening, after his long flight across the high seas, and resting for the night among the grass-covered ruins of some city of the jungle over which a monarch, centuries dead, had once held sway. It would be only poetic justice for him to enjoy the posthumous hospitality of a vanished empire, while in a bare apple tree to the north a bundle of grasses, tilted more than ever, now, and capped with a little mound of snow, remained as the last monument of his own temporal sovereignty.

LORENZO

Lorenzo

THIS account of Lorenzo, in the nature of a memorial, is occasioned by his death. Only yesterday, sitting at my desk as I am sitting now, I was aware of that hard yellow eye, like the eye of conscience, overlooking and appraising my work even before the ink was dry. I believe that Lorenzo's presence on the perch above my desk had a salutary effect on what I did. Sitting there, stalwart and unmoved as he always was, he reminded me constantly of the fact that the world at large would be little affected by any achievement of mine, but that it would wither me like my own conscience in case of failure. That little eye would observe me with a steady impartiality for hour after hour, page after page of work; but it could, on occasion, contract and intensify its critical light like a flame. Even yesterday morning there was still no sign to show that some inner malignancy was sapping the strength that fed that light, and bringing Lorenzo, minute by minute, closer to his end. Death was sudden, for it can never be otherwise. No matter how long we have watched its approach—and with Lorenzo it was a matter of months—we are always mercifully kept from realizing its imminence till there it is; and then all is over.

I had known Lorenzo so well, and for so long, having lived in daily contact with him for more than two years and traveled thousands of miles over land and sea in his company, that I knew it instinctively when, several months ago, his robust body began to be undermined by the stealthy trouble that brought about his end. I could recognize illness, but I could not recognize death till it had been accomplished; and even now its seems hard. I cannot remember that he is gone, and when I look up for his comment on what I have just done, that empty place is always a shock. It is not easy to believe that those last retching gasps for breath, accompanied by cries so unlike any his voice had produced in life, were final. It is not easy to harbor such a thought because I find it impossible to fix in my mind that fatal instant in which the living Lorenzo was divided from his dead body. Even after the last cry, when he lay on his back with eyes still bright and beak half open as though the voice were still within, he seemed alive. Only later, when the final rigidity of death had set in, when the wings became constricted against the body, warping its shape till it looked as though it had been rolled through a mill, was it possible to recognize death.

In the face of a universal destiny that unites us all it seems strange that our direct predecessors on earth, who were more concerned with immortality than with the temporal present, should have given thought to the survival only of men. Yet they conceived of men as a kingdom in themselves, separated from the animal and vegetable worlds by a capacity for spiritual existence that made them worthy of grace. Because of that spirituality, so hostile to the body, it was reasonable to believe in disembodied survival for men. To us, who are no longer so sure of our souls, it is impossible to avoid taking notice of the physical, historical, and even temperamental characteristics that join us to the rest of the animal world. The body of mankind now seems to grow from the

universal body of nature in company with the other varieties
of animal life, and the separation is so indistinct that we
cannot credit it and must rather suppose links in the chain
to have been lost somewhere along the abandoned route
of progress. And now that we have conceived life as a natural
entity which must survive intact or not at all, we can no
longer believe in the supernatural element that formed the
better half of the dual cosmos in which the ancients lived,
and made death inconceivable to them. To us the world of
nature is a vast brotherhood of similar and related forms,
in which man is one among many; but the supernatural
world that might have given it meaning has disappeared
from before our eyes. Immortality, which might now have
extended to all nature, no longer exists for us.

Today Lorenzo does not sit on his perch as I knew him,
looking down on me with his unfaltering gaze. All those
things that gave me so much pleasure in him, the aloof and
aristocratic demeanor, the strength with which he could
lift a whole apple up in one great foot and hold it aloft
without effort, the offhand fashion in which he would occasionally bite out a piece and grind it to pulp between his
powerful mandibles, all those characteristics of his that
aroused my half-humorous affection and esteem are gone.
Nothing more is left of Lorenzo than the remembered
images that prompt these reminiscences.

Lorenzo first came to my attention in the tropical lowlands of Central America which are the native home of his
species. In that part of the world, between the volcanoes of
the Sierra Madre and the Pacific Ocean, the species is the
commonest of all the parrots and the most highly regarded
as a pet. It is known to the natives as the *loro real,* the royal
parrot, because of the yellow crown that rests like a large

gold-piece on the nape of the neck. Scientists have given it
the taxonomic name, *Amazona auropalliata*. I have also seen
specimens in museum cases labeled, Golden-Naped Parrot. From lower Mexico to Panama on the Pacific coast you
may see these big birds, morning and evening, flying in pairs
over the jungle, or discover their forest rookeries by following the clamor of their hundreds of shouting voices. Lorenzo, if his had been the normal fate of the species, might
still have been one of these, flying at dawn and again at
dusk with his mate over the luxuriant roof of the forest,
fighting with rivals, feeding on outer branches a hundred
feet above the ground, finally mating and raising his young
in the hollow interior of some dead giant of the jungle.

But the beauty of form and color, the intelligence, the
adaptability to a foreign environment, and the vocal powers
of the species have made the *loros reales* desirable as human
companions. Lorenzo went directly from his nest, which
must have been in some more than ordinarily accessible
tree, into the world of men. He never knew and he never
missed the wild way of life that had been the lot of his for-
bears. Exactly how he was taken I cannot say. Some Indian
with an observant eye had seen the parent birds coming and
going at the nest-hole and heard the food-calls of the young.
Either he climbed the tree at the proper time with a piece
of sacking to wrap the young in or, if the hole was inaccessible, he cut it down with his machete. The father and
mother parrots may have set up a great hue and cry, diving
at the marauder to frighten him off, or they may have melted
silently into the woods like crows when their nests are mo-
lested by men. In any case, the Indian got at least one very
bewildered and frightened fledgling, covered with a thick
coat of white down through which its new feathers were

already pushing; and in the manner of young birds, I suppose, it crouched down in the sacking and tried to make itself as inconspicuous as possible.

Lorenzo's earliest memories were of an Indian family living in a thatched hut on a hillside where they cultivated the corn from which the woman made the tortillas that they shared with him. This much I know, and more, from what Lorenzo said afterwards. A very young baby, less than a year old, lived in the hut and was nursed by the woman who, when she went out about her work, carried it in a shawl over her back. Lorenzo used to perch on the ridgepole of the hut, or in the shade trees that grew alongside it, and listen to the incessant crying of the infant, the thin wailing that would not end till it was finally exhausted and could only gasp for breath. There was also a boy named Bepo. In the evenings, when the smell of tortillas rose deliciously from the fire inside the hut, the woman would come out front and call Bepo in to his meal in her shrill voice. I see her there, in the doorway of the hut, her hands on her hips, shouting, Bé—po, Bepo, Bepo, Bepo, Bé—po, with the accent heavy on the first syllable. The family gave Lorenzo his name and taught him to say it as they did, sometimes affectionately—as one might say, good Lorenzo, sweet Lorenzo—at other times in the long-drawn syllables that are used for shouting: Loré—nzo, Loré—nzo. . . .

There are gaps in Lorenzo's history that will never be filled now. I do not know how it was that he came into the company of the Indian with whom I first saw him. The man, taller than most of his race, thin and morose, was a smuggler who carried on his trade in cigarettes and small trinkets across the frontier between two republics; and therefore he must have been more enterprising than his fellows. Some

strain of Spanish blood, going back to the days of the con-
quistadors, may have accounted for his decision to abandon
the traditional ways of his kind in order to better himself.
I judge that he either bought or stole Lorenzo from his
home; and since it would have been simpler merely to take
him when no one was present, the latter is probable. In any
case, he had not had Lorenzo in his possession long enough to
win either his fear or his friendship, for he carried him on a
stick held out in front, as though afraid of being bitten if
he held him on his hand.

I had been sent out along the line by the railway company
for which I worked to check up on the labor gangs that kept
the road-bed in condition. In that country the recurrent
floods and hurricanes, and the tropical vegetation which can
smother the traces of man in a few weeks, make keeping the
line open a constant and unending struggle against the
powers of nature. Road gangs of eight or ten men, under a
caporal who maintains the prestige necessary to his authority
by remaining idle, labor continually along every section of
the road. Occasionally young accountants in the capital, restless like myself after too many weeks in the office, leave the
comfort of the city and spend a few days traveling over the
line in an open gasoline motor to check up on the work gangs
and make sure that all those listed on the payroll are actually
on the job.

It was still early morning and the sun had just risen
when we stopped a few miles short of the frontier to examine a *caporal's* list. The laborers were lined up alongside
the tracks for us to count: one, two, three, four, five, six,
seven, eight, nine; and nine names on the list—*bueno,* all
was well. As we were about to go on we saw the morose Indian approaching along the tracks ahead of us, a bundle

over his shoulder and Lorenzo sitting, like a falcon un-
hooded for hunting, on a short stick that he held in his hand.
The man eyed us narrowly before he came up to offer his
contraband. My companion, who for three years had smoked
only the harsh native brands of the region, immediately began bargaining for cigarettes; but my attention was fixed by
the parrot. *Que bonito!* He was a *loro real,* stalwartly built,
with large and powerful feet (I noted his points with what I
like to think was the eye of a connoisseur), broad shoulders
supporting an immense, heavy, square head that seemed to
contain all there is of wisdom and disenchantment. His near
eye, which was examining me as closely as I was him, was
bright yellow, with that lustrous, jewel-like quality that his
eyes always had, to the moment of his death and even after.
The condition of the plumage was good (though not as
nearly perfect as it was to become later), a bright green body
with glossy sheen on the wings, yellow tail, a large yellow
disk on the nape of the neck, a tinge of blue across the top
of the head, and flight feathers (which I could just see under
the folded wing) black and yellow, bright blue and brilliant scarlet. He was distinctly a noble bird. The dignity of
royalty sat well on his powerful frame.

"How is this bird called?" I asked the Indian.

"He does not have a name, señor."

"Do you care to sell him?"

The morose face of the Indian attempted a disparag-
ing smile, as though it would never occur to him to sell
so excellent a creature. Part with such a bird?—perish the
thought! . . . If the señor cared to suggest a price, however.
. . . He lifted his shoulders. No harm in a little bargaining. . . . A moment later I had taken a dollar bill from my
pocket and Lorenzo's person was committed to my care, to

follow me and dwell with me wheresoever I might go, till death should us part.

I cannot say that Lorenzo and I really grew to know and understand each other during those first few months of our association. In fact, the honeymoon was difficult for us both. His dignity and reserve, and my impatience, made a long period of trial the condition of our friendship. There were frequent regrettable displays of bad temper on both sides. Lorenzo, when I wanted to make my goodwill manifest by stroking him, would draw back, squawking with alarm, his foot absurdly raised to fend me off; and if I persisted he would snap at me with so much purpose that he invariably drew blood. I felt that he was betraying my better nature. I resented the fact that my friendliest advances were the cause of his greatest hostility, and felt that there was something willfully perverse in his choosing to regard the gestures of seduction as threats of rape. And the invariable result was, of course, that I ended in the role he assigned me, not infrequently, to my immediate regret, by cuffing him. We often sulked for days at a time and would have nothing to do with each other. I blame the smuggler for our unhappiness. That the family in the hills were kind to Lorenzo I know from the affectionate way in which they spoke his name, but his distrust of me must have been a direct reflection of mistreatment at the hands of the man from whom I bought him.

In the capital city, a day later, Lorenzo had his first chance to examine the works of man in their magnitude. He saw buildings of stone and plaster, with one story piled on another, paved streets through which automobiles hurtled, and dense crowds of people. But, to my disappointment, he was not impressed. He looked out upon the scene through expressionless eyes, as though it were part of the normal environment to which he had been brought up. He merely accepted it all. The city existed, and therefore could not arouse in him the wonder or the awe that would have depended on a belief in the possibility of its non-existence. He could not greet it with philosophical wonder or poetic rapture because he could not conceive the void that might have been. There it was, and because it was he accepted it. Illusions never had any part in Lorenzo's world. Things either existed or they didn't exist; and if they didn't exist they could not enter his consciousness. That is why he never foresaw death, or knew it when it came. Recognition of eternity, of the possibility of negation, would have utterly shattered his placid belief in the existence of things.

It is fair to say that Lorenzo made a far greater impression on the city than it made on him. When I walked down the street with him on my finger, the passers-by would pause to murmur *"chulo,"* or *"bonito,"* before they hurried on. Lorenzo never said anything on such occasions, unless he grumbled a bit under his breath to indicate an awareness of his surroundings. In the godlike impartiality of a consciousness that entertained no questions, he was the undoubted superior of the fallible human beings who paused instinctively to estimate his value and comment on it. What he knew he knew immediately and without a doubt.

The first mirror Lorenzo ever saw was on the chiffonier of the room that he shared with me in the capital. In that mirror was a parrot, a large and handsome parrot, that sat on the finger of a person who appeared to be the exact counterpart of me. I suppose he accepted the fact that I should have a double as he accepted everything else. But a fellow-parrot—that was a different matter, requiring a vigorous response. Immediately, without forethought or hesitation, Lorenzo ruffled up all his feathers and struck. The other parrot, which had suddenly become much larger and fiercer, struck at the same moment. If he had drawn back, like any normal bird in the face of a sudden attack, Lorenzo would have known what to do. But this parrot was a different sort of reality, a new and aggressive reality that could not be frightened. Instead of following up the charge, Lorenzo drew himself back and raised one foot in the air to ward off the counter-attack of his rival—and the rival did likewise!

I think the only moment of philosophical uncertainty Lorenzo had in all the years of his life was in front of that mirror. For the first time he met a reality on which his intuitive responses had exactly the opposite effect from what might have been expected But it did not take him long to discover his mistake, to find out that it was not an ordinary parrot he had to deal with; and, if no ordinary parrot, then no rival! As soon as he had grasped this fact he lost interest in his image. He accepted it as he accepted the room he was in and the finger that supported him, as he accepted the fact that when I pressed a button there was light, when I pressed again there was darkness. It belonged to the order of things that require no response.

The wood on top of the mirror, where Lorenzo perched, was something else again. But how could I be angry at him when, a few days later, the landlord pointed out to me in vigorous terms that the irreplaceable maple frame had been largely eaten away? I paid for the damage silently, in Lorenzo's presence. A being whose outlook is so positive, so integrated, that it goes beyond the dualism of human understanding to a Nirvana in which, because everything is equally good or equally evil, there is no good or evil, is above either praise or blame. It is easy, in this light, to see why our ancestors found no place for the beasts in an after-world where punishment and reward are meted out to saints and sinners. It was only man that fell from grace in the Garden of Eden.

Those first few months were vexatious in more ways than one, for circumstances never left us long in peace. Still, I must be grateful for the irregularity of our lives, since the foundations of our mutual regard were laid at that time. Since we had been through so many trials together, and had endured the buffets of travel over a wide area with faith in each other's fortitude, it was inevitable that our attachment should in time become firmer than any that might have been cemented in the course of a placid existence. At the end, only death was stronger.

We had not been a week in the city when the call came to move to the capital of the small neighboring republic. Lorenzo was placed in his traveling box, an old gasoline-tin with a perch fastened diagonally across it, where he lived for two mortal days, bumping about at my feet on the floor of a little railway carriage that rattled horribly uphill and down till it finally arrived at our destination.

Our room on the second floor of the hotel overlooked one of the two or three central squares of this other city (it is a city of squares). Two windows led out to the narrowest of balconies, from which the room was separated only by two pairs of glass partitions that swung in and out, like saloon doors, with wide gaps at top and bottom. Lorenzo's station was on one of these, where he could sit the livelong day looking out over the little park in which vultures and men moved busily about their appointed tasks amid green trees and statuary. At one end of the park, directly below, was a

taxi-stand at which were displayed, as in a museum of an-
tiquities, the worn-out remains of the early automobile age.
Any parrot with a taste for color and movement, for live-
liness (and I never knew one without it), could find all he
wanted here. Every few minutes the appearance of a possible customer in the entranceway of the hotel would give
the signal for a mad contest. Motors would roar, spitting
flame and barking like engines of perdition, gears would
grind, as the antiquated taxicabs swung out of place and all
converged simultaneously on the goal. Private cars clamped
their brakes and swerved desperately out of the way; pedestrians fled for their lives. There were frequent collisions and
enough street-fights to entertain a Roman Emperor, let
alone a new arrival from the country.

Lorenzo quickly won the sympathy of the taxi-drivers. He
sat there at his window all day like a fairy princess im-
prisoned in a tower by a colossal dragon, and morning and
evening called out his name in tones so plaintive that they
would have melted the heart of the most hardened sinner,
as though calling for some worthy without fear and without
reproach, some noble Don Quixote, to ride to the rescue and
slay the monster. When nobody came, he would sometimes
launch himself out into the air and flutter down on his
pinioned wings into the middle of the street, among the
moving automobiles and absorbed pedestrians. Immediately
there would be a hue and cry among the drivers—parrot
overboard!—and a rush to see who would be first to the
rescue. It not infrequently happened that, returning from
work in the evening, I would be met half a block from the
hotel by one of the drivers carrying my Lorenzo perched
on his finger. I like to think that even now Lorenzo's memory
cannot be completely lost in that city.

But the greatest of our trials, our first enforced separation, came after we had been there almost two months. One early morning the traveling box was again got out and Lorenzo placed inside for the return journey to that city in which he had first contemplated the works of man. At the railway station the conductor stopped me as I was boarding the carriage of the train, the box with Lorenzo inside swinging from my hand. The following scene Lorenzo observed through the square windows that had been cut in his house, but he made no comment.

"I am very sorry, señor, but this time the *loro* must go into the baggage car. I must follow the regulations." The conductor was a good scout and knew me as a fellow-employee, but he felt constrained to be on his strictest behavior because the traffic manager was, by misfortune, standing near by. "If the manager will grant his permission . . ." He nodded in his direction. I turned to my friend the manager, having no doubt that I would find him as obliging as usual, and made my request. But the presence of the conductor required a good example. (If the mighty are unrighteous, how shall the weak know the law?) Lorenzo was relegated to the baggage car up front, where all that day, while he had dinned into his ears the monstrous snorting of the locomotive, he waited without food or water for whatever fatality might be next on the program of his existence.

At the little village where the train stopped for the night I approached my fellow-worker, the station agent. Together, like thieves in the dead of night, we crept through the darkness of the railway yard to where the train was sleeping, and with the aid of a flashlight made a hole in its side and rescued Lorenzo from his imprisonment among all the huge shapes that loomed obscurely, like shades of the infernal regions, over his little traveling box. But we could give him only a short respite. That night he sat on the shutter-door of my bedroom, eating fresh bananas, but in the early hours of the morning he was restored to his prison.

Tragedy struck upon the hour of our arrival in the city. I had left the train as soon as it entered the station to greet some friends whom I had not seen in several months and, when I returned, the baggage car, with Lorenzo inside, was gone. Desperate inquiries brought forth the bad news. The worst had happened. The car had already been taken to the *aduana,* the custom-house, to be examined. Lorenzo, my Lorenzo, had fallen into the clutches of the Supreme Government, the dread "Gobierno" that one mentioned only with awe, and by this time he would be entangled in such a network of red-tape that it was doubtful whether he could ever be extricated. There was no time to blame myself. Hurriedly a phone-call was put through from the station to the agent of the railways at the custom-house, and the case presented to him in all its tragedy. Here was a parrot, gentle, affectionate, and of noble demeanor, utterly devoted to a master who, in turn, would pine away in his absence. Interned among strangers who obeyed a law higher than themselves, he would doubtless die in his captivity, starved by regulations and strangled by rules. What could be done to save him?

The agent knew the answer, and it was as I had suspected. Nothing could be done, nothing at all, now that the bird had arrived in the *aduana.* There were other parrots to be had, and, well, in time one forgets. . . .

Early the next morning I went down to the *aduana* with the resolve to perish sooner than fail in the rescue. I waited with others on a bench in the outer office till my friend the railway agent came out to me, a jolly fellow with a trace of Negro in his skin and features, who would, I believe, have remained imperturbable through a universal cataclysm. Kindly and generous soul that he was, he recommended fortitude, the stiff upper lip. We would all do our best, he said, in the manner of Nelson admonishing every man to do his duty. Then he left me.

The hall in which I waited was spacious and dusty, pervaded by a constant roar as though it were the interior of an immense hive in which swarms of insects fanned the air with their wings. Clouds of white dust rolled in from the street through the open portals at one corner. Running along the far side was a series of cages giving access to the offices which sheltered in their midst the inner sanctums whence the great and mysterious drama of Government was directed. Somewhere behind that barricade of steel cages sat the sinister symbolic figure who held power of life and death over my *loro*. Ranged on the benches, or lounging against the walls, were all the innumerable hangers-on of the invisible Government, a motley crowd of scribes, clerks, and others whose strange function it seemed to be to remain motionless but alert all day, observing the scene closely through half-shut eyes. They stood against the wall or sat on the benches, barefooted for the most part, with ragged pants that bagged at the knees, with dirty linen coats, with battered straw or felt hats, and waited for the drama to unfold. The quietness of the scene was a quietness of suspense, as though attending the imminent revelation of the Day of Judgment. There was an air of some immense importance lurking secretly overhead, ready to strike and never striking. In the tension of the atmosphere you could see how men, their nerves tautened by time, straining for release, might in sheer desperation resort to revolution.

As the day advanced, it became hotter. One took off one's hat to fan oneself, or wiped the sweat and the dust from one's face with a dirty handkerchief. Factotums with white caps would come out into the hall, bristling with the significance of their roles, address a few words to some hanger-on, and disappear into their cages once more. Before the morning was over I knew them all, the squat half-breed with the aggressive military mustaches that belied a face seamed with anxiety, the thin man with the narrow head and hard mouth, the plump fellow with the abrupt manners. . . . I knew them all, the talkative and the silent, the quick and the slow, the tall and the short. Occasionally one of the benchers would rise, go to a gate in a cage and say a few words, then return to the bench to wait with eyes fixed on the ceiling, on the floor—anywhere so long as it was nowhere. A woman in a black shawl with a black pigtail over her shoulder came in from the open, got quite hysterical about something, and was led ungently out again by one of the white-capped factotums.

The agent came back to see me. He had been working hard, he said, matters were advancing. He was trying to arrange an interview with the third assistant customs-master, and I must not be impatient. I must wait, wait. . . . Again he disappeared into the cage. He returned later on, and this time I followed him down a long corridor to the office of the third assistant. He knocked on the door and listened. There was no answer. He knocked again, touched the handle, and then turned it cautiously. The door opened and we both slipped in. A sallow man in a white cap, with a long, thin nose, a mouth that turned down sharply at the corners, and cheeks drawn in as though he were perpetually sucking on them, sat opposite us marking papers at a heavy mahogany desk. He raised his eyes to take us in, then lowered them and went on with his marking. From the distance came the faint humming of bees, but in the room was silence, broken only by the scratching of the pencil and the faint sound of our breathing. Finally the figure at the desk looked up again at the agent, who was standing in front of me, and waited with pencil poised for him to speak.

"This is the señor," said the agent, stepping aside to reveal my presence, "who has the *loro* that is being held."

The official moved his eyes to my face with automatic expectancy, and waited. . . . It was up to me now. I took a firm grip on myself and began my story in what I intended to be a casual, man-to-man tone. I understood—as who wouldn't?—that it was not possible for foreign parrots to enter the sovereign territory of the republic. But this parrot of mine, it should be observed, was a native whom I had bought in the country. He was, I said, searching for his sense of humor, a good citizen of the republic. (But my little joke fell on barren soil. The third assistant customs-master did not care to take notice of it.) I drew a breath and went on. He must understand that one was fond of parrots, one grew attached to them. Take this *loro* of mine, for example (while we were on the subject of *loros*), a fine healthy bird, bought at a great price, and in the country. I had traveled extensively with him. He was a pet—he was, in fact, my only pet. He was the only pet I had! I drew another breath (that made two) and paused for a moment to allow him to take in the full implications of the words. It was increasingly difficult to go on. The man's black eyes remained fixed on my face with a look of infinite vacuity. I resumed my monologue, trying to move him by raising my voice and becoming increasingly eloquent. Naturally one was anxious about one's pet, I said. One's heart was troubled. Such a fine bird too, much attached to me, and undoubtedly at this moment, at this very moment, pining away among strangers who did not understand his needs. One was naturally anxious. . . . It was all such a regrettable error! I should never have taken the bird out of the country had I not been a foreigner ignorant of the Regulations of the Republic. At this point I began to find difficulty in breathing at all. The parrot was healthy, I continued. But one was anxious. He was a native bird. He had been purchased in the country. . . . He was healthy. . . . And he was my only pet—the only one I had. . . . One was anxious. . . .

My eloquence finally collapsed completely under the silent stare of those dark, empty eyes. It was like addressing the wall, or the mahogany desk. After another long pause, in which the agony of our embarrassment was almost visible, my companion found his voice and managed to pronounce, weakly, that I had a parrot that was being held in the *aduana,* and that both he and I would be thankful if the Excellency could see his way clear to releasing it.

The third assistant customs-master turned stiffly in his chair to face the agent, and at last spoke, though the opening of his lips was almost imperceptible. "Have you presented a petition?" It was the first time I had heard the sound of his voice.

"No, señor, we have not."

"Then there is nothing more for me to do. Good day." He returned to his marking while we moved away to the door, both of us murmuring *"muchisimas gracias,"* and escaped into the corridor.

A petition meant all sorts of delay and expense, but there was no choice. Back in the outer hall we bought two sheets of the specially stamped paper required for the purpose, and hired a professional writer of petitions—one of those benchers—to draw it up. The scribe was a little bare-footed half-breed with a battered fedora. He passed his tongue over his lips as he listened to our business. This petition, he said, would be a weighty matter, requiring much thought, much thought. The phrasing must be just so, and not otherwise. But, trust it to him, he was a man of sense and experience, he would know how to attend to it—at a price. We made the arrangements as though we were commissioning the man to paint my portrait or do a battle-piece for the National Museum, and left him with the understanding that we would meet again in the afternoon. It would, of course, take him several hours to complete the work. Then I went off to cancel my reservation on the airplane that left the city the next morning. I should have to wait over till the threads of Lorenzo's fate had been unraveled.

In the afternoon I returned to my bench of atonement, and after half an hour the writer of petitions came in with the two stamped sheets covered in small but elaborate script that looked as though it had been copper-plated. The first page and three-quarters of the petition consisted of polite and formal addresses to the Excellencies whose mercy was sought. They were exquisite, but beside the point. The last quarter-page implied that there was a *loro* being held by the *aduana* whose return the undersigned begged the favor of. I affixed my signature and left the petition at the gate of one of the cages. There were no further developments that night.

By the middle of the next morning the petition had been

examined, and the agent brought it out to me at my bench in the big hall. The factotums who acted for "El Gobierno" would not read it, he said, because the proper kind and number of stamps was not attached. I went out and bought some more stamps, pasted them at the head of the paper, and again left it at the gate. In the afternoon, when I returned, the agent met me with a downcast face. He was afraid our case was lost, hopeless. He had done everything possible. Now there was only one chance left, a slim one. The second assistant, who was a good fellow and an acquaintance of his, would see me later. Meanwhile I must wait patiently and be of good cheer. There was no hope!

The afternoon wore on, unmarked by any change in the continuous hum of activity, the buzzing of bees. The benchers sat quietly and morosely, like horses at a cab-stand. At last the agent came out to me with the white-capped second assistant customs-master. He was a short, rotund man of uncertain age, with the face and manners of a cat. His cheeks were soft and round and sleek, and a long drooping mustache sprouted from below each nostril. His little eyes were canny, dangerous and good-humored at once. Before proceeding to business, he shook hands with me ceremoniously. It was perfectly permissible, he said in soft purring tones, to enter *loros* into the country. Perfectly permissible. There were no regulations against it. No regulations. There was no difficulty, no problem at all. All this fuss, his voice seemed to imply, how vain! No need of it really, no need at all. I felt myself admonished by his tone.

In a humble voice from which I tried to exclude the relief I felt I asked: "I may take the *loro* now, then?"

"There is first of all a formality required. . . . A formality, a natural precaution," he added, as though defining the word. "Merely a safeguard, you understand. The bird must be examined by a medico from the Ministerio de Agricultura."

"Can that be arranged?"

"Ah, señor, *quien sabe,* who knows indeed?"

"Would it be possible, señor, for me to remove the *loro* to the Ministerio for the purpose of the examination?"

"No, señor, that would not be possible. That would be impossible. Your *loro* must remain here till he has had his examination, and then you may have him, then you may remove him."

"Will it be possible then, señor, to have a medico come here from the Ministerio?"

"That, señor, is your own affair. I cannot help you."

He shook hands once more, made a little bow, and retired from the field, leaving the agent and me again murmuring *"muchísimas gracias"* and wondering what to do next.

"You will have to give up hope for your *loro,*" said the agent, in the tone of one who breaks bad news gently. "The Ministerio will never consent to send a medico here. One would hesitate to ask them."

At my urgent request he finally consented to phone the Ministerio and see what could be done. The Ministerio listened to his story and gave its decision that so weighty a question could not be settled over the telephone. Again, there must be a petition. "El Gobierno," like the fearsome dragon of fable, must have its maw crammed with petitions and more petitions, with specially stamped paper at fancy prices and flowers of speech by the pageful, before it would bend its ear to an ordinary mortal. One did not transact business of magnitude over the telephone.

"But that will take another day at least," I almost shouted as soon as the agent had hung up, "and I have to catch the airplane tomorrow morning. Already I have waited two days. Already all my plans have been upset. Mother of God, what more do they want now? Must I buy a robe for the Madonna in the Cathedral before I may have my little *loro*? And meanwhile he is doubtless starving. Tomorrow he will be dead."

Upon my feverish insistence he called the ministry again and explained that the matter was urgent. I must say for him that he made a really eloquent plea, and the upshot was that they suddenly agreed to send their medico right away.

An hour later the doctor arrived on a bicycle from the Ministerio. He was a tall man of middle age, very American in appearance, and behind his horn-rimmed spectacles was the first truly friendly face I had seen in two days. "I'm sorry you were kept waiting," he said in fluent English as we shook hands. "All this fuss must seem an awful nuisance to you. Let's have a look at your bird and get it over with."

We walked out through the portals together and down the dusty road to the shed in which Lorenzo was stored. "Been in this country long," he asked, "or are you a newcomer? . . . Of course we haven't yet got things as well organized here as they are in the States, but we're working toward it. Give us time. I've lived in the States myself for years—took my medical degree at Stanford."

Lorenzo's tin box was standing forlornly on top of a pile of crates in a dark corner of the shed. Coming in from the brilliant sunlight of the street, we at first had difficulty distinguishing it in the gloom. We took it out to the doorway, where I uncovered it, half expecting to find merely a bundle of feathers instead of the live bird. But there he was intact, sitting placidly on his perch after two days of darkness, as completely unperturbed as though it had been the immemorial custom of his kind periodically to shut themselves away from the world in darkness. I was there, so why should he be surprised? It was all in the nature of *things*. He climbed slowly to my finger, pulling himself up with his beak, shook his feathers loose, stretched one wing over one leg, and mewed with pleasure.

"Hello, Lorenzo," I said.

"Lorenzo," he answered. "Rrrrrrrrr."

The doctor glanced at the bird, his healthy plumage, his noble eye, and passed him. "I bet you've had the devil of a time trying to get him out of here," he said.

When I left the *aduana* I carried Lorenzo proudly on my finger. He was an incomparable bird now, tenfold more precious to me since I had fought and bled for him. His existence was the plain manifestation of my mercy, and I loved him for it.

I think this episode marked a turning point in our lives. I flattered myself, in the emotion of the hour, that as a result of the steadfastness I had shown in his service he began for the first time to distinguish me favorably from the morose and doubtless cruel Indian who had been his previous master. Some obscure understanding, which was in time to become a firm bond of sympathy and affectionate regard, united us. From then on I respected his right not to be stroked against his will, and, reciprocally, he left off his affectation of alarm and his attempts to bite my finger whenever I approached too close. In our silent and undemonstrative way, we understood each other.

It is therefore a matter of regret that our association had to be broken so shortly after its greatest triumph. But it would not have been fair either to Lorenzo or myself to ask him to accompany me on the expedition I was about to undertake, to share discomforts beside which those we had already endured would appear luxurious. Our cases were, after all, different. I could not expect Lorenzo to partake of that sense of adventure which, in civilized man, will soften the hardest bed and make coldness or heat, dampness or drought, a strange and intoxicating delight. Man, with his sense of illusion, his knowledge of the void, his uncertainty of himself and the universe which impels him occasionally to put both to the test, can endure pain with pleasure and suffering with exaltation in the deceptive search for the reality of things. Having conceived the void, it must be his constant endeavor to fill it in by the pursuit of knowledge that reveals both himself and the world. And the satisfaction of that impulse, which by a ludicrous understatement is ordinarily called curiosity, is the justification and reward of his pains. But Lorenzo had no curiosity. His was a practical soul that functioned only in a pragmatic world. The knowledge he needed to cultivate his garden came to him easily through instinct and experience, and the boundaries of that knowledge, conforming to the boundaries of his garden, were fixed and absolute. He never went beyond them. He never adventured against the void. To have taken him along on an expedition that administered only to the satisfaction of my own human needs would have been to inflict needless hardships upon him.

The alternative was better. On one of the broad cobblestoned streets of the city stood a mansion, a noble plaster edifice two stories high with patios and balconies; a place of comfort and a luxurious enough shelter for any parrot. The master of the house was our common friend, one of the first acquaintances Lorenzo had made in his new life. Recently bereaved of an excellent macaw, he was anxious to welcome Lorenzo to his place in the family circle and extend to him all the hospitality of a prodigal host to an honored guest.

I have reason to believe that Lorenzo was very happy during his stay in this home. For once he was living the normal life of a parrot in the city, surrounded by friends and admirers, free to sit all day on the rail of the rear balcony, munching tortillas and watching the clothes that fluttered on the washline. He saw the baby of the household take its lessons in walking, up and down the balcony, its mother supporting it under the armpits while it struck at the floor with its feet and gurgled with pride in the manner of all babies, white or Indian, country or city. The fat Indian servant-girl with the black pigtails used to bring him nuts or bananas as a special treat, and stand beside his perch while he ate, murmuring in gentle and passionate tones, over and over, *"Lorenzo chulo . . . Lorenzo chulo . . ."* so that no parrot could fail to feel immensely flattered. Often the baby had long spells of crying, always a delight to Lorenzo's ears, and then he would respond with his own masterful rendition of the theme as he had first learned it in his home in the lowlands. There was also a little white dog in the house who gave Lorenzo the opportunity to exercise his superior dignity. The little dog had a habit of making playful rushes at the parrot, leaping into the air like a woolly lamb, and yelping with joy. But the parrot would fix him with one coldly glittering eye, his head cocked so that he could look down on the creature below, and finally the dog, made suddenly self-conscious, would slink away into a corner and hide. Lorenzo always regarded himself as the equal of human beings, and as such above servile caninity, which he invariably put in its place with his withering glance of scorn.

Gradually Lorenzo began to broaden his horizons in this new city life. A visit to the adjoining house, belonging to a soldier, was always well repaid. In the early morning you walked along the railing of the balcony, slowly and with stately deliberation, head lowered in advance to feel out the way, placing one foot before the other crosswise on the bar with due forethought for each step, since it does not become royalty to appear hurried or eager for the feast. At the end of the railing an iron bar ran up to the gutter overhead. You examined the bar for a moment, estimating its firmness and tensile strength, then lifted one foot and placed it tentatively in position. This accomplished, you reached up with your beak and grasped the bar tightly between your mandibles. Then, by contracting the muscles of your neck, you hoisted yourself up and placed the other foot on the bar. From this position you reached out with your beak and got another hold higher up, pulling yourself up in this manner till you came within reach of the gutter, when you hooked your upper mandible over its edge and let go simultaneously with both feet. This maneuver was always sure to arouse the admiration of any observers who might be watching from below. You hung there by your beak for a moment, and then slowly lifted your two feet together till they grasped the edge of the gutter; from that it was a simple matter to pull yourself up to a standing position on top. Here at last you could allow yourself a few carefully chosen expressions of satisfaction in the achievement. You might ruffle up your feathers and say, "Hello, Lorenzo," or purr gently, before you lowered your head and proceeded once more with the same deliberation along the gutter to the house next door. Arrived there, you found another vertical bar by which you could lower yourself to another balcony in all respects like the first.

The soldier had a mistress with flowing raven hair whose practice it was to sit out on the balcony in the morning quite obviously awaiting the arrival of the *loro* from next door. Occasionally the soldier himself, who had grown rather stout with the years but wore the most beautiful polished leather boots, would come out onto the balcony in his shirtsleeves and suspenders and address the woman in a high-pitched and querulous voice. That was always great fun, for then the woman would return the soldier's addresses in tones that were still higher and still more querulous; and so they would vie with each other until, as often happened, the woman would suddenly begin to sob, just like the baby when it had been crying and could no longer catch its breath. But she was always most affectionate to Lorenzo when the soldier had gone back in, putting her face, with its delicate scent of perfume, close to his and murmuring all sorts of endearments in an infinitely sweet and melancholy voice, quite unlike that she had been using for the man. Once, however, in the evening, she sat on the soldier's lap, right there before him, and quite shamelessly used the same terms of endearment to him that she had to Lorenzo; and then Lorenzo got violently jealous, ruffled up all his feathers, spread his tail, and uttered long, dismal roars of rage—to which, in her wantonness, she paid no attention at all!

But when the sky began to grow dusky Lorenzo always returned along the gutter to his perch on the balcony of the other house, for that was, after all, his home.

Meanwhile, in the contentment of his new life, Lorenzo had forgotten me entirely; for he never took stock in what was not immediately present to his senses. To Lorenzo's host, who was a human being with the strange capacities of his species, I continued as an illusion in the vast, unfathomable stream of time. But Lorenzo had no sense of time and no illusions. Beyond the two houses, the patch of sky, the wash on the line, the dog, and the people who surrounded him, was nothing, not even the void.

I must admit that there were so many things to occupy my consciousness during those weeks that I, in turn, rarely thought of Lorenzo. He belonged to the past which, in so crowded a present, I had little leisure to contemplate. I imagined him to have taken firm root in the affections of his new hosts, and was content that it should be so. But the weeks went by and one morning I found myself in a little port on the coast, preparing to embark in a few days in a steamer bound for New York. As living mementos of my sojourn abroad I had already collected Maria and Pedro, so that Lorenzo was no longer the only parrot who had a claim to my consideration. Maria, a *loro colorado* that dazzled the eye with brilliant greens, blues, yellows, and scarlets, was a bumptious hussy with a high squeaking voice. It was her boundless delight to be manhandled, rolled over on her back with feet in the air and tickled all over, tossed from hand to hand, twirled over one's fingers. She would shriek with excitement like a schoolgirl, call out her own name in a spasm of ecstasy, and finish with gales of hysterical laughter. In absent-minded moments she had a way of clucking to herself and whistling coyly. Pedro was a small and nervous edition of Lorenzo, without his golden symbol of regality. He was possessed by some demon who pricked him intermittently to fits of violent activity. He never moved at all except under the spell of a *crise de nerfs;* and then he went off like a bomb. He ran along his perch, swung down below it, hanging by his feet, beat his wings against the unresisting air, and opened his beak to vent loud squawks of terror. He was as unhappy in his nature as Maria was happy. But neither possessed the high serenity that distinguished Lorenzo, the nobility of his bearing, the slow, deliberate articulation of all his movements. They were, in a word, ignoble. For them I could feel affection and pity, but not the esteem that belonged to him alone as the repository of a soul which rose loftily above the ignominious conditions of its existence. They were my ordinary playthings, to be toyed with, to be caressed, to be patronized; but Lorenzo had, in the vicissitudes of our association, made good his demand to be treated with all the respect that I should expect myself. He taught me not to question his dignity as a fellow-creature. Maria and Pedro, those clowns whom I still cherish with affection, can never take the place in my regard of the being who had become, more than my pet, my associate.

It was not certain that Lorenzo could reach me before my boat sailed. However, I promptly dispatched a letter to his host in the city asking that, if it could be done without inconvenience or the breakage of hearts, he be placed on the train immediately. He arrived the evening before our sailing, was taken out of the baggage car in his little tin traveling box, and delivered into my hands, his feathers unruffled and his soul unstained by the wear of the journey.

And now that I once more existed, he recognized me. He climbed up onto my finger without fear or suspicion, knowing from previous experience that its support would not fail him, and once there shook his feathers and gave voice to his pleasure. He mewed, he murmured, he called his name and wept a bit; and finally, to put the seal on his demonstration, he sang a little song he had learned from the Indian woman in that forgotten hut on the hillside. It was a very little song. I heard him sing it only two or three times in all the days that I knew him, and then always with a modulated joyfulness that expressed his perfect and sublime contentment with the order of creation.

The next afternoon I strode up the gangplank with three tin boxes of parrots and set foot on the deck of the ship that was to take us all out of the tropics into a world where human beings were common but parrots strange and rare. The purser, a little round and red-faced cockney bursting out of the seams of his white duck uniform, bustled up under the canvas awning and blocked my entrance to the companionway. "Wh-at do you think you're doing with them birds?" he asked. "Tike them off again, right away." He struck a belligerent attitude, as though to show me that I need not judge his importance by his size.

"These parrots," I said, "are traveling with me to the States. They belong in this ship."

"If that's what you think it's about time you learned that you can't tike parrots into the Stites. Now, go along, tike them back where they come from. I won't be 'aving the blasted birds in this 'ere ship." The little man's face had become a glowing red, from the fat throat that burst through the opening of his collar to the roots of his hair. "Tike them away, I s'y, tike them away. This ain't no bloomin' parrot-'ouse."

"If you don't mind," I said, "with the permission of the officials of your company I shall do nothing of the sort. I have made arrangements for their admittance into the States, and I have arranged with your superiors for them to travel in this ship. You asked what I thought I was doing with them. Now you know."

"Well, you didn't ask me, and I won't 'ave it. So now *you* know." He squared up to me as though to suggest that I knock a chip off his shoulder. What Lorenzo must have thought of such a ludicrous little man, had it occurred to him to pass judgment on any manifestation of creation, I hesitate to think. Mercifully he chose merely to disregard him. The fact that he existed did not even merit an exclamation point.

The day was very hot, and I was anxious to get below and settled in the ship, but I had to reckon with that obstruction in the companionway. "If you will step about one pace to the left . . ." I ventured, "I will be able to go below."

"I'll see those bloody birds in 'ell before I step aside," he shouted. "And I'll see you tike 'em there too. Mike a bloomin' parrot-'ouse out of the ship, will you? I'll step aside, I will! Oh, yes, I'll step aside!" He danced and fumed under my nose, crowding against me like a little ship bearing down with all her canvas spread. Granted the power of Lorenzo's eye, I might have sent him slinking into the corner merely by looking at him, as my partner had looked at the dog when he threatened to infringe on his dignity; but I was not so gifted. I had to fall back on the Law, in the shape of our captain, who appeared on deck at that moment.

"What's the matter, here?" he asked, addressing the purser.

"I've been telling this 'ere gentleman," he responded in a surly but subdued voice, "that 'e can't tike 'is parrots to the Stites aboard of this ship, sir. And 'e says as 'ow 'e can!"

"I have obtained the permission of the company and made all the necessary arrangements," I said. "But your purser seems to think the decision rests with him."

"We'll leave them aboard now and discuss the matter after we sail. Let it go at that, purser."

"Well, 'e couldn't do it if you didn't s'y so, sir," the purser murmured, removing his bulk from the entrance to the companionway.

That evening, at sea, the captain called me up to the bridge and gave me my orders. In our next port of call I was to visit the American consul and swear out before him an affidavit in which I attested the various qualifications of the birds for entrance into the United States. With that paper in his keeping, the captain could allow Lorenzo and the other two to continue the journey.

The American consulate of the little port at which we called the next morning was situated at the far end of an embankment lined with royal palms. I looked at the brass plaque beside the door of the house, which assured me that our consul, Mr. E. F. Hargraves, kept office-hours from eight to eleven. It was ten o'clock when I rang the doorbell. A lanky black boy with long arms and big hands that hung limply in front of him came round the corner of the house to the steps of the veranda and looked up inquiringly at me. "Wha-a-a' you lookin' foh? Mis' Hargraves ain't git up yit."

"Will you tell him I'd like to see him?"

"He ain't git up out of his bed yit, suh."

"Just tell him I'd like to see him anyway, if you don't mind."

"Well, he ain't git up yit, but I'll see." He disappeared

through the screen door into the house, and in another few minutes I began to hear distant sounds of scraping and shuffling and grumbling from deep in the interior. There was a sudden clatter, as if a chair had been knocked over, and then the slow, distinct, and well-rounded utterance of a curse that, from its nature, evidently applied to the untimely visitor. After some more scuffling came the voice again: "Harry, you go on out and tell that unmentionable son of perdition to go walk in the ocean. Then get me a cup of coffee." The Negro came to the door again. "Mis' Hargraves, he's jist gittin' up, suh. He says you'd better come back in 'bout an hour."

"If it's all right, I think I'll wait inside." I went in through the screen door and sat down at a table littered with a vast disarray of old magazines. I had just finished an article on the value of our foreign trade with Latin America when a figure clad in a wrinkled suit of green-striped pajamas and a frayed bathrobe appeared in the curtained doorway at the far end of the room. It was a robust, hairy-chested figure (as I could see through various gaps in the suit). The dense black hair of the head was in confusion, the face was haggard and dusky for lack of shaving, the eyes were bleared, and there were still discolored patches along one cheek where it had rested, but a little while ago, so snugly against the pillow.

"Yes?" Mr. Hargraves inquired brusquely, scratching his chest with one hairy paw. "What do you want?"

"I'm sorry to break in on you like this," I began, "but my ship just got in this morning and may leave during the day. I have three parrots that I'm taking to the States——"

"Parrots!" he exploded. "Is that what you want to see me about?"

"Yes," I continued. "I have to swear out an affidavit in order to take them on board ship. The captain says——"

"Come this way," he interrupted, making a visible effort to contain himself, and led the way through the curtained aperture to his little office. A monstrous, old-fashioned typewriter stood on a desk littered with papers and cigarette stubs.

"Now, what do you want to swear to?" he asked, seating himself before the typewriter and rummaging on the desk for a sheet of blank paper.

I specified what was necessary. He made a distinct attempt to control his indignation, but it was no good. "And why the hell, may I ask, do you have to take those birds up to the States? Can't you get parrots that are good enough for you up there? I never saw the like of it. Making all this fuss for a couple of worthless birds, as if you couldn't just as well buy them in the States—if you've absolutely got to have parrots."

"These particular parrots," I said gently, thinking of Lorenzo, "are special friends of mine."

"Well, there's no accounting for some tastes! Don't mind me! If you've got to have them I suppose you've got to have them!"

"That's right," I said.

When I left the consulate half an hour later I carried with me a paper, stamped with the seal of the United States of America and bearing the signature of her representative, grudgingly attesting the importance of Lorenzo, Pedro, and Maria.

The Odyssean stage of Lorenzo's career terminated with his arrival in the United States of America. Having known five nations, having followed the sea, having traversed the dark jungles of tropical lowlands, scaled mountain-tops, and lived under the ominous shadows of immense volcanoes, having crossed a continent and gazed upon the two great oceans of the globe, having visited the largest city and some of the least—it was at last time for him to settle down to that sessile existence in the halcyon harbor which is the dream and the abiding hope of all adventurers. But here I am indulging the pathetic fallacy, for Lorenzo never took adventure as seriously as men do. Life, which he had been given the opportunity to experience to an extent equaled by few parrots in the history of the race, never invaded his integrity or made any lasting impression on his memory. He was never awed by size, humbled by distance, or amazed by the amazing. For him the stars shone in vain, and the world, except as it ministered to his needs, remained always below the level of his consciousness.

The arrival of Lorenzo in New York should properly have been a major turning point in his life. As a bird (though it is stretching a point in favor of science to consider him so) he possessed that instinctive knowledge of space and direction that has always baffled men, who must invent compasses and a variety of gadgets to compete with it. Therefore I take it that Lorenzo, perched in his tin traveling box below decks, knew the course of the ship as well as our captain. When he arrived in New York he knew he had ventured beyond the limits that mark the normal geographical experience of his kind, into an alien and unfamiliar world. I looked forward to the drama and incongruity of that moment when he should step from his box to contemplate the greatest concentration of humanity in the history of our globe—the immense buildings, the roaring machinery of New York—

as I might have looked forward to the moment when, a rocket from Mars having fallen into my backyard, a Martian stepped out for his first view of Earth. Would he be awed . . . or would we? I pay my greatest tribute to Lorenzo when I record that the issue did not remain in doubt for an instant after he had emerged onto my finger and shaken his heavy feathers loose. "Lorenzo," he said and, reaching for a nut, calmly ground it to bits in his bill.

If one judges an organism by its adaptability, its capacity for adjusting itself to changing conditions, the group in which Lorenzo had the privilege of membership must be given a high rating. Obviously a parrot is above the immediate condition of his surroundings. Unlike so specialized an organism as the everglade kite, for example, which feeds exclusively on snails of the genus *Ampullaria,* he is all but omnivorous. He stands independent of any one source of supply. The kite is the slave of the snail. He must confine his range to the few fresh-water marshes of this world where *Ampullaria* lurks. His habits must be governed by the habits of *Ampullaria,* which comes to the surface and exposes itself to capture only in the early morning and late evening. His temperament must be limited by the narrow bounds of his activities. If some plague should suddenly destroy the genus on which his livelihood depends—and plagues are a feature of nature—it would likely be the end of the everglade kite. His bill, and probably his internal economy as well, is suited to little else besides the devouring of these snails. His species, like a nation that has come to specialize in one product, could not be insured. The chances are too great that it is a passing phenomenon.

But I doubt that mankind will see the end of the tribe of parrots. Surely, when the earth has become a frozen waste of rocks, when the sea has dried up, when the sun no longer shines and the only relics of man are a few white bones mingled with the dust of the mastodon, the stars will still look down on some green Lorenzo of the future, perched contentedly on a block of lava and cracking pebbles in his bill! There, in the transcendent placidity of the Lorenzos of this earth, is immortality for you!

It is hard to believe that death could touch a being whom nothing in life could seriously disturb. Untroubled by the vicissitudes of a precarious and unpredictable existence, safe from the danger of being unnerved by knowledge—what could death do to such a one? I fondly believed that Lorenzo would be receiving the admiration and esteem of my successors long after I myself had achieved the end that awaits all mortals. And when his time came, I supposed, he would confound the powers that be by taking death in his stride, as he took everything else.

Since that date when I finally bowed to Lorenzo as a superior being the better part of two years has elapsed; and today he is no longer with me. I have taken his perch down from the wall above my desk because I would not impose its emptiness on my memory. I had got into the habit of looking up at that perch whenever I came to a pause in my work to see what Lorenzo thought of what I had been doing. When I was worn out, the strength of his imperturbability refreshed me. When I had doubts, the composure of his bearing reassured me. When I knew in my heart that what I had done was bad, but hesitated to recognize it, the steadfastness of his eye gave me courage to scrap it and do it over. He was a rock in every storm, a symbol of fortitude in the midst of chaos. As the months went by and the bond that united us was gradually strengthened, I grew increasingly proud of owning his friendship; and owning it exclusively, for he accepted no one else. He did not give himself easily, and to establish our association on a lasting foundation of esteem and affection after years of mutual restraint was an achievement in which one could take satisfaction. Pedro was nervously incapable of sustaining such a relationship. His spasms of terror from within fed his suspicious hostility and misanthropy. Maria gave her confidence readily, with perfect trust in the beneficent intentions of all the world, but at the price of her dignity as an independent creation, a sovereign empire in the vast, ungoverned universe. One condescended to her whims, but one did not respect her. Neither of them had the aristocratic demeanor, the inner dignity, and the self-respecting independence that made Lorenzo worthy of being honored. He knew his value, and you took him on his own terms.

Lorenzo found little difference between his new home in the northern country and the Indian hut of his youth. He was never a mere scientist to multiply distinctions. His position was, rather, analogous to that of the artist who rises *au dessus de la mêlée* to find universal principles in the confusion of apparent diversity. To anyone with such godlike perspective the resemblance between human beings, whether civilized or savage, reduces their differences to insignificance. The woman who plays bridge is the sister of the woman who cooks tortillas; both are Woman, and when that portentous word, which contains in its two syllables as much of awe as men may know in this life, has finally been uttered, what can be added? Even had he estimated persons and passed judgments on them I doubt that from his place in the universe he would have noted anything below our universal characters. He might have perceived that the Indian smug-

gler (cruel and ambitious outlaw) and I (gentle and governed) differed as individuals, but he would have considered,
rightly, that we belonged to one all-embracing class. I could
have taken my shoes off and shouldered a pack without
causing him surprise; and the Indian, without seeming to
deviate from the normal, could have put on a necktie and
sat down at my desk to write this story. Even the respective
tongues in which we speak are, to a Lorenzo, mere dialectal
variations of a common language.

By the same token, Lorenzo never distinguished the
birches in which he climbed outside our house from the
trees in which he had perched at the edge of the jungle. It
did not matter that these were poor stunted growths next
to some he had known. He was concerned with their universal use, not their variety, and from this aspect they bore
an absolute resemblance to the maple frame of that mirror
in the capital. The fact that they were wood, and as such
suitable for sharpening his mandibles, was enough. He proceeded with thoroughness and deliberation to prune them
the moment he was placed in their branches, and so effectively that he had already done away with two good trees
before I knew it.

In some measure our respective interests overlapped and
we could co-operate in their pursuit. It is a habit of long
standing with me to go about the countryside with a pair of
binoculars to observe the birds. Lorenzo was also an observer of birds; but a reasonable observer, not in the indis-
criminate manner of his partner. The small fry, the ordinary cheeping creatures of the bushes, did not concern
him. A robin, though he landed alongside, danced a horn-
pipe, and sang the *Liebestod* in F-major, would not have
got so much as a passing glance of interest from him. Such

organisms administered not to his comfort nor did they threaten his security—to what purpose, then, should one look at them? Hawks were another matter. There he shared my interest wholeheartedly, and with better reason than I could claim for myself. I don't suppose that in all his career he had ever been actually menaced by a hawk; but he understood their threat with that intuitive knowledge which is the wisdom of the generations. His race, since the obscure beginnings of their struggles in the tropical forests of the past, had learned to be wary of the hunter, and had passed that wariness on to him along with the store of accumulated experience to which every nestling parrot is heir. He could disregard the somber crows that his ancestors had never seen, but little falcons half their size, which to the unenlightened observer seemed as harmless and attractive as butterflies, immediately put him on his guard. An airplane roaring low overhead would go unnoticed while Lorenzo stared with steadfast and unblinking eyes at some buteo circling so high above that he was invisible to human sight.

And in our common preoccupation Lorenzo had all the advantage. Often I knew of the presence of hawks only on the evidence of his concentration, for however hard I strained I could not see them. Distance was done away with in the piercing gaze of that hard yellow jewel in its green setting. The sun, blazing with all its brilliance in a livid sky, could not repel it, and I should be tempted to say that Lorenzo regarded even the sun as an equal—if I did not know that as a matter of fact he regarded it not at all.

These feats Lorenzo accomplished with one eye, against my two. But in respect to his entire visual equipment he had an added advantage. At most I could include only a small part of the sky in one view, and was constantly having to shift my gaze back and forth over its expanse to discover the migrating hawks. Without seeming to look anywhere, he saw everything. The merest speck above the horizon in any direction would catch his attention though he had not turned his head to find it. In this he was superior to the hawks themselves, for their eyes, like those of owls and men, are fixed in one direction. Hunters that they are, they look forward and forward only, for much the same reason that Christian wore armor which covered only the front of his body when he went out to do battle with Apollyon in the Valley of Humiliation. What hawk is there that needs to look back over its shoulder? But those that are hunted must see behind as well as before if they are to survive. They must have eyes projecting from both sides of the head that nothing may escape their notice. Lorenzo, I believe, could see the entire circle of the horizon, the ground below, and the sky above without turning his head.

Now that the season of the fall migration is approaching I shall miss those field trips of ours more than ever, for in the observation of hawks I am once more thrown back on my own limited resources. Of course there is Pedro (Maria is away at a neighboring house), but Pedro is capricious and unreliable; it is just like him to point a dragonfly and pretend it is a hawk merely to bear out his belief in a world full of terrors. I shall miss the dependability of an infallible observer. I was used to going out of doors during the hawk season, when the wind was fair and a clear sky promised a good migration, and calling Lorenzo down from the trees. He was always eager for a walk, and would immediately come climbing down, lowering himself from branch to branch till he finally dropped down onto my extended hand, purring with pleasurable anticipation of our expedition. Like parrots in their wild state, his favored perches were invariably on the outermost twigs of the treetops, and his method of descent was to move out till his weight bore his perch down to within reach of another twig one stage below. Grasping this firmly with his beak, he would follow with his feet, dropping down on it and swinging below to the next twig. His progress was deliberate and invincible, like the slow progress of a spider descending from a height on an invisible filament spun from its body. But, however long it took, nothing would distract him from his set purpose. He had none of the capricious uncertainty of petty minds—of butterfly or bandarlog—that decide on one course one instant and another the next. When he had made up his mind as to the proper course, nothing could turn him from it.

We walked back over the big hill with the windmill on top, down through the woods, and out into the swampy Meadows. Lorenzo sat upright on my hand, attentive but at ease, observing nothing and seeing everything. It was enough for me to watch him. . . . Suddenly his head would be cocked on one side, one yellow eye looking up into the transparent sky. My gaze would immediately follow his, straining until it found its object, one lone speck circling or floating down the wind; or sometimes a whole cluster of specks like water-bugs against the blue. Then Lorenzo would be moved to my shoulder and, like the mere man I was, I would raise my glasses to search for the characteristics by which I might differentiate genus and species, age and sex.

These walks always promoted an added intimacy between us. Lorenzo liked to be scratched at any time. When I approached him he would lower his head till his beak rested on the perch between his feet and allow me to ruffle the feathers along the back of his neck and scratch the delicate pink skin beneath them. Oh, the ecstasy of it! He would close his eyes and let his soul float away in a dream of bliss while wave after wave of rapture passed through him. Then he would raise his head, eyes still shut, so that I could scratch under his throat and about his heavy jowls. But on these walks it was permissible to go even further. Then I might rub down the hard glossy feathers of his back, smooth out his wings, and pull his tail. He had finally come, in the course of our association, to have complete confidence in my respectfully affectionate interest.

But it was Pedro who brought forth in its most vivid manifestations the true nobility of Lorenzo's character; for it is in choler, rather than in love, that nobility is most expressive. I must admit that the first time the two were brought together Pedro, by a freak of his nature, got the better of the encounter. Lorenzo was approaching him along a branch, slowly and with rising anger, when the demon that possessed Pedro pricked him to one of his sudden spasms of senseless terror. He might just as well have rushed in one direction as the other; but by chance he made a dash straight at Lorenzo. This was unexpected. Lorenzo halted in his tracks, lifted one foot in the air to fend off the attack, and then retreated, snorting with indignation. His dignity would not allow itself to be compromised in a rough-and-tumble with such an irrational creature. A bird that launched an attack with so little ceremony was not a worthy opponent.

Lorenzo's method was different. When he went to do battle he first engaged in a formal ritual that gave significance and drama to the event. The overture was a series of

deep roars or growls, one after the other in rhythmic se-
quence. The feathers of head and neck were raised, the
wings were lifted out from the body at the shoulders, the
tail was spread in a bright yellow fan bordered with green.
As passion rose new motifs began to weave into the theme,
shrill screams and long-drawn decrescendo wails; but the
roars of rage continued like the awful drumbeats of fate
throughout the performance. Then the war-dance began.
He bowed forward on his perch, lowering his head and raising his tail, righted himself again, drew himself up, and
lifted one foot to make threatening passes in the air. And
all the time his war-cries were increasing, growing louder
and fiercer, till terror seemed to pervade the entire landscape. At the climax the wings were stretched out full above
the back, like crimson standards of battle. Then he began
the fearful march, slow, deliberate, invincible, pausing now
and again to bow and lift his foot in the ceremonial gestures
that were calculated to strike terror into the heart of the
enemy. He advanced dancing, like an African warrior in
full regalia, his featherdress shaking over his head, moving
to the sinister beat of war-drums and the frenzied wail of
battle-cries. Pedro had retreated to the farthest end of the
tree, where he stood uttering little anguished squawks of
panic. But it was no good. The march continued, slow and
inevitable, from branch to branch, like destiny. When Lorenzo arrived, finally, within reach of his victim there was a
sudden commotion of rending squawks, and then he struck
with gaping beak. Pedro, driven mad with terror, jumped
from his twig and fluttered to the ground below. And then,
what was Lorenzo's triumph! Wings spread out—blue and
yellow and scarlet—head raised and feathers ruffled, he
danced a great dance of victory over the fallen body of his

opponent. He screamed with passion, he roared with right-
eous wrath, with pride he shouted the dread syllables of his
name, dancing first on one foot and then the other; while
Pedro waddled meekly off through the grass to another tree
where he could perch in safety.

In time Lorenzo came to tolerate Pedro's presence in the
same tree as long as there was no serious provocation; but if
I made any advances to Pedro, spoke kindly to him or looked
at him with benevolent eyes, then he began his war-dance,
and woe to Pedro if I did not retire immediately! He could
brook no rivalry to his regality.

With the passage of the seasons, however, Pedro came
to have one advantage over Lorenzo. Both parrots had had
their wings clipped when I first got them, and though Lorenzo's had grown back in, certain essential flight feathers
remained missing. But in the course of successive molts
Pedro became a strong flyer and began to spend his days
like the wild birds, flying about the countryside, feeding in
the fruit trees, and returning only in the evening to become
a domestic parrot once more. Lorenzo would watch his
antics in the air with a sort of helpless indignation that a
creature so far below him should be granted a power of
which he himself was shorn. Then he became bitter, like
Samson in Gaza, and sometimes roared with rage and disappointment.

By and large, however, he led a contented existence. I
don't think he ever missed the power of flight in itself, for
his kind are not primarily flyers but climbers in the treetops.
It is strength of foot and beak, not strength of wing, that
gives distinction to the parrots. Even the wild parrots ordinarily fly only in the mornings, on their way to their feeding grounds, and in the evenings on the return journey to

nest or rookery. Their flight is clumsy, slow, and laborious; and during the greater part of the day they remain in the food trees, climbing from branch to branch. Lorenzo's normal life was not seriously affected by his inability to fly.

Certainly Lorenzo suffered no ignominious captivity. He retained all his independence of spirit, living with me as was his pleasure, receiving the food and shelter that were his due, and in return conferring the inestimable favor of his goodwill. The serenity of his mind was rarely troubled. He dwelt always in those higher realms of the spirit which the greatest philosophers among men have struggled vainly to attain. He took no more notice of our winters, for example, than if they had been the normal condition of his existence, and though he came indoors during the coldest weather he would ride out a snow blizzard on his swinging perch in the treetops as if it were nothing more than a beneficent tropic breeze. He did not so much adapt himself to circumstances as rise above them. His character, in the dignity of its self-regard and the serenity of its temper, as well as in its splendor when roused to anger, might have served as an inspiration to wayward and faltering mankind. He epitomized life at its best, primitive, virile, and transcendent.

Yet there is a destructive power moving in all of us that transcends even life. We are all united at last, parrots and people, in the destiny of our common mortality. The disease that sapped Lorenzo's life first became apparent many months ago in a swelling that indicated the presence of some morbid growth within the framework of his body. There was nothing that could be done about it. Gradually, as the weeks passed, he talked less, forgot to call for Bepo in the morning, to roar at Pedro as he flew past. But the advance of death was so surreptitious that it remained imperceptible to the end. He still purred and grumbled to express his unchanged contentment with the order of existence. I kept him often indoors, on his perch above my desk, and I can testify that his eye lost none of its brilliance. Like a strong man in his old age, reduced once more to the conditions of his childhood, he slept more than had been his habit, and sometimes his breathing was labored. But he retained to the moment of his death the loftiness and untroubled assurance of his demeanor, against which it seemed impossible that death could prevail.

It was only on the last evening of his life that he showed any sign of weakness. A sudden spasm came over him during which his wings fell limp and he had difficulty in keeping his perch. But it lasted only a moment. In the morning he seemed as well as ever again; less active, perhaps, but calm and contented. I gave him an apple which he held upraised in his powerful foot while he bit great mouthfuls from it. His appetite, which was always large, was not diminished by the approach of death. But I heeded the warning of the day before, and in the afternoon I got out his old tin traveling box, neglected now for almost two years, to take him for a visit to a man who had lived all his life with birds and understood their ailments. It was the first time since his arrival that Lorenzo left home, and he never returned.

The entrance to the naturalist's domain was by a rutted dirt road that ran alongside a pond in which a variety of ducks, geese, and swans swam sedately after their group-leaders, like little bands of serious students being conducted about a museum. The road turned sharply away from the pond and led up to an irregular wooden bungalow whose various wings projected at random.

The naturalist heard me drive up and came out of the screen door of his office to meet me. He was a large figure of a man, ponderous and slow-moving, and yet with a certain ease in his bearing that made him seem not at all ungraceful. The weight of his years sat well upon him, and in his face was that indefinable quality that is found in men who have spent their lives in close association with the primitive, a reserved quality of humorous kindness different from the sentimentalism that comes so easily to people who know nothing of nature, more sure of itself and at the same time less demonstrative. Holding Lorenzo's box carefully in one hand, I followed him indoors and down a short hallway to his office. A soft, modulated sunlight made its way through the window on the other side of the room and lighted up one of those solid and everlasting monuments of furniture with which a generation now gone gave expression to its faith in the future, an immense mahogany table with square, carved legs. Along two walls, at the level of the ceiling, was a row of glass doors through which stuffed ducks and owls standing on wooden perches looked down with bead eyes upon a scene that had not, one imagined, altered in its appearance since the opening of the century. They stood there immovable and expressionless, like symbols of eternity.

"You find me," said the naturalist, "as usual, surrounded by birds. And now, your bird . . . Let's see what we can do for him."

A space was cleared of old journals and magazines on one corner of the table and the box placed on it. I could hear Lorenzo stirring inside, his feathers brushing against the tin walls of his old prison. When I removed the cover he climbed out slowly and ponderously onto my finger. But now one could see his weakness. The effort to pull himself up tired him visibly, and for a moment he breathed with difficulty. The naturalist looked at him with an appreciative eye. "He's a fine specimen. But that little swelling . . . let me see. I'm afraid that's bad." He clucked ominously under his breath and searched about the papers on the table for a probe. Lorenzo eyed him suspiciously with that hard yellow eye of his, and when the man reached out to grasp his tail, holding the probe in his other hand, he gave a squawk of indignation and opened his beak threateningly.

"He doesn't like to be handled," I said, anxiously. "You may have trouble."

There was less trouble than could have been expected. Lorenzo struggled bravely to pull away, lifted his foot to keep the threatening hand back, and tried to reach it with his open beak. But now the weakness had him in its grip. He made an attempt to call out, he thrashed about, and suddenly he no longer had the strength to defend his dignity. His voice broke pitifully and his breath failed him. The man had relinquished his tail, but already it was too late —death was launching its final attack. The bird began fighting for air, gasping noisily through his wide-open beak. Then his wings came loose and his convulsed body fell over sideways on my arm.

For an instant I had been taken by surprise, but now, all at once, my heart turned over inside me. "Oh, it can't be," I exclaimed, "he can't be . . . !" Up to that fatal moment I had never really envisaged the possibility of Lorenzo's death. He was always such a stalwart, imperturbable being, so sure of himself, so steadfast in the assertion of his own independence! And now, suddenly, this frightful spectacle, this degradation! In that moment when the truth

broke upon me it was not my own loss I felt, it was the terrible humiliation of Lorenzo's weakness, the crying shame of
it. He lay in my lap now, gasping for breath, and could no
longer protect himself. Those eyes that looked out bravely
on the world in every direction, those eyes which nothing
had hitherto escaped, could not have seen the coming of
this cowardly invasion from within. Shame, shame, that a
being in whom all this dignity of life resided should be
brought to such an end, struck down from behind by the
invisible enemy!

I don't know what visions of the past rose up before
Lorenzo's eyes in that last, desperate moment. He was
already beyond me, on the frontier of a world from which
no being has returned to bear testimony. But it all came
back to me: Lorenzo as I had first seen him on that tropical
coast, riding on his perch like an eagle on a standard of
battle. The glittering rails stretched away to a fine shim-
mering thread in the heat of early morning, and along
them came the morose Indian bearing Lorenzo to a chance
encounter whose outcome no one could then have foretold. Lorenzo in the city, serenely superior to the comments
of the admiring pedestrians: *"Loro chulo, O qué bonito!"*
Lorenzo calling plaintively from his station overlooking the
little square, attracting the attention of the taxi-drivers who
called back to him from below. Lorenzo the Steadfast, climbing out of his tin box in the gloom of the custom-house shed.
Lorenzo the Invincible, challenging Pedro with colors flying. . . .

And now he lay in my lap, gasping, gasping. I held him
close and could do nothing. He made a last effort to regain
possession of himself, struggled up once more to a standing
position on my finger. He could still fight for the integrity

of his being. But the life was slowly, relentlessly being choked out of him. His gasps became frenzied, his wings fell apart, his head with the beak strained wide open bent slowly back on his shoulders, farther and farther, wrenching backward till he fell over again into my lap. Finally the retching gasps grew weaker, separated by intervals of silence. The eyelids closed up halfway over those brilliant jewels, the body became slowly rigid, the feet stretched out convulsively, motionless, grasping the air. And then, when the struggle was over, when death had won its final, irrevocable victory, there came in succession from that gaping and lifeless beak three terrifying peals, three rending shrieks in an unknown voice that seemed to cry out in a last enduring agony of despair against the shamefulness of mortal existence, destined for such an ignominious end. The void closed over the last scream and cut it off. . . .

I lifted the dead bundle of feathers quietly and placed it on the mahogany table. Neither the naturalist nor I uttered a word for several moments. We were both silent, embarrassed and shamefaced, like two men who have together and in privacy witnessed a spectacle of the most abject degradation and share forever a secret of shame that they dare not put into words. Death, which had just destroyed a bird, touched us both.

When, after a few minutes, we found our voices again (for the silence had become unendurable), it was of inconsequential things that we talked, of birds in general, of the weather, of anything and of nothing. All the while the dead bundle lay between us on the table like some unmentionable substance, but we kept our eyes raised and pretended to disregard it. When I finally left he saw me out to the door, and there, just as I turned away, he ventured some expression of sympathy, murmured something that I caught as I was walking down the gravel path: "I have seen this happen so often . . . I know how you feel. . . . I understand. . . ." Yes, I thought to myself, I shall miss him. All these months, and now . . . But it was not my loss that I felt, it was Lorenzo's final disgrace, his dignity and independence brought ignominiously to the dust.

It is unavoidable that in an obituary notice of this sort one should tend to exalt the character of the deceased, to fix his memory by giving it an importance that in the scheme of things as they are it could never have had. Lorenzo was, after all, only a bird. His individual death, like his individual life, meant little. He was only one of countless specks swarming over the surface of this earth that carry on the vital spark through the generations; one that became isolated by fortuitous circumstances from the main stream of its kind. He lived his life not with other parrots but with human beings, sharing with them the comforts of their existence as though the association had been a part of the order of nature. And one, at least, was benefited by it.

To complex minds, capable of subtle perceptions that, if they are not guarded against stalwartly, may destroy the integrity of the world, to minds that live always under the threat of the abysmal void, the companionship of the primitive can be a great comfort. For the primitive mind has that strength and serenity in the face of a hostile world which the complex mind is always in danger of losing. It opposes the stress of inimical circumstance like a rock in the midst of a raging stream. Lorenzo, like all primitive life, human or animal, lived exclusively in the present. He had no knowledge of the nature of change, of growth and inevitable decay. For him every moment of existence epitomized eternity, every object was steadfast, every sensation enduring. He had no invisible enemies, because what was not visible did not exist. He foresaw no end to creation.

I like to believe that Lorenzo retained his invincibility even in death. His greatest failing, from the human point of view, was the source of his greatest strength. He had no sense of humor, he could not recognize the existence of what was absurd. He lacked intelligence, even the intelligence of crows or dogs, but he had that primitive wisdom which rises above curiosity and doubt. His outlook on the universe was invincible because it was everlastingly positive. He never judged anything. He accepted equally everything that was presented to his senses. He found nothing wanting in existence because the possibility of non-existence never presented itself to his mind. A recognition of the primal chaos, of the abyss, would have made him an easy prey to death. But life can never suffer by what it cannot experience, and so it is impossible to believe in Lorenzo's extinction.

I see him coming at last into the dark underground caverns of Erebus, to the vast gloom where Proserpina sits sadly on a black throne beside her somber spouse to receive the departed souls that chaos could not consume; and the spectacle of so vital a creature, unhumbled by its translation to the realms of death, recalls to her memory the bright splendor of life which she shares anew each spring. She takes him on her finger and, while he shakes loose the gorgeous feathers of his wings, watches him with that melancholy, half-humorous mingling of awe and affection with which we on earth had regarded his immutable existence. Perhaps strange, eternal music is playing softly; but he does not hear it. Perhaps, as a mute offering of admiration to the invincibility of that life, the Queen of the Underworld tenders him a grain of corn that she had secreted in her robes at the time of her latest visit above. He cocks his head on one side and fixes the kernel with that glittering yellow eye. "Lorenzo," he affirms; then, as the music swells to a whelming climax, he reaches out for it and slowly, with the serene deliberation that will never leave him through eternity, grinds it to bits in his bill.

BIRDS AGAINST STONE MEN

Birds against Stone Men

LOOKING from the top of the ridge across the pale sea of banana fronds, the face of the jungle seemed to rise in a high escarpment curving back on either hand, a black peninsula of forest jutting into a pale green ocean. A shelf of cloud behind it hid the rising sun whose rays had already whitened all the upper sky. The silhouettes of giant trees broke through the jungle, anchored by threadlike cables of liana that hung straight down from their heads. Far off to the right, near the base of the mountains on the southern skyline, a winding strip of bush marked the course of the river whose annual overflow had for many millennia impartially abetted man's struggles to survive here and, in the intervals of his defeat, the countermarch of the tropical rainforest. Inert and torpid in the heat that had begun to make itself felt with the sunrise, the forest yet dominated the landscape like a boundless darkness that would again seal up the bright opening men had made, and not for the first time, on the valley floor. Already today there is talk of abandonment. The work of holding the danger back is beyond the endurance of men, their courage at last exhausted with the passage of the centuries and the fulfillment of all their hopes except the ultimate desire for rest. Inch by inch, day by day, the forest closes its wounds.

I clambered down through the wet grass of the bank to the ocean floor, entering a vaulted colonnade made lumi-

nous by the greenish light that fell through thin banana
fronds overhead. At the far end I found the passage abruptly
sealed by the lower jungle, a wall of fernlike growths, still
glistening with the morning dew, and cohune palms whose
immense fronds sprayed upward from their stems in ample
arcs. The buttressed bases of the major trees rose through
them to another world, the upper forest which could be
seen only in glimpses far above. Somewhere beyond that
wall was a clearing that communicated with the outside
world by a trail entering the woods a mile away; but it was
part of my purpose to be there before the heat had imposed
silence on the birds of the forest. I knew that the constant
din from the interior, the cooing and croaking, the howls,
the laughter, and the whistles, would in another hour begin
to give way to the comparative stillness of the tropical midday, when the birds move so quietly in the foliage that they
are hardly to be found. When I came on a breach where
the banana-cutters had felled a tree I advanced into it without stopping for thought.

In the dark interior the grasses and ferns closed overhead
and obstructed the way with their stalks. Suddenly I was as
small as a rabbit. A series of buttresses climbing out of sight
against the wall of a tree made a sharp detour necessary,
mere roots were almost insurmountable. It would never do
to get lost here. This new world, like some underground
cavern into which I had stepped as casually as Alice had
fallen down the rabbit-hole, was not a human world. Plants
that utterly dwarfed a man grew up from the floor and hung
in masses from above like green stalagmites and stalactites
—and there were other forms of life whose continual movement I heard behind the foliage. But these were not my

woods. I advanced, one step at a time, till something zoomed past me, remaining noisily just behind my shoulders. When I turned, a green hummingbird hung vertically in front of my face. Immediately it began to circle about me in a series of darts, pausing in the intervals to scrutinize me from every angle: it studied the front view, the three-quarters view, the side view, and the back view, occasionally darting up closer to confirm some doubtful point in my appearance. So this was Man! In return I got a clear impression of the hummer, its long surgical beak decurved into a quarter-circle, two white feathers pendent from its tail. But this was only one jewel detached from the endless recesses of the cavern. A grassy plant that looked like swamp grass magnified a hundred times, with a crimson and yellow bloom forming a geometric pattern, was evidently a kind of wild plantain. But I did not know whether a fern fifteen feet high was a fern at all; I merely nosed about its roots, like a mouse, and gave up. A giant butterfly, painted azure, flapped its way out of one dark passage only to be swallowed up in another. When I heard water being poured from a bottle in rising musical cascades high overhead I knew the big Montezuma oropendulas were about the top of the forest. The other sounds, the slapping and barking, and the continual spattering as though it were raining in big drops somewhere in the upper stories, were a mystery.

It was easy enough to advance through the forest—I had become so small that I could walk under grasses and ferns without stooping—but the repeated necessity of making detours about the foundations of trees was confusing. Before I had gone forty paces I turned abruptly to retrace my steps while there was still time. . . . But already it was too late.

Now I found the forest extending unbroken over the area where, a few minutes before, only the wide expanse of banana plantations had been.

Suddenly I knew I was lost. The ground beneath was black loam, soft and springy to walk on, but too elastic for footprints, while overhead the tangle was so dense it hid the sky. The massive tree-trunks presented a solid bank of orchids and parasitic plants impartially on all sides. No matter which way I turned, the dark, luxuriant, motionless masses of vegetation rising from the loam on clustered stalks seemed equally favorable and equally hostile to an advance. I began to run through the monstrous underworld of the jungle, stooping low and paying no attention to direction. I ran blindly, as in a nightmare, deeper and deeper into the jungle the more I tried to escape it, till in another few minutes, as abruptly as I had been lost, the jungle delivered me up again at the clearing I had originally set out for. Confronting me face to face was the life-size stone image of a barbaric personage who sat, cross-legged and immobile, in the gaping jaws of some vaguely defined but terrible fanged monster.

Pieces of sky showed again through openings above, the same reassuring sky that stretches over the banana fields. I fell back against a tree to rest, facing the stone man in his attitude of immovable dignity, as if sitting in judgment, his enormous headdress of plumes and masks unruffled. In his right hand he held a scepter, symbolic of his authority over a people who had long since fled from these woods to leave him alone before the wild plant and animal life which knew no human law, still grasping the insignia of his vanished sovereignty in the midst of the wilderness. Beyond, on pedestals of carved stone in an open parklike glade that had been cleared from the jungle, stood other images in stone regalia, images more than twice life-size, their bare faces somber, their lips thick, their features soft and heavy, surrounded by a riot of stone plumes, of grotesque animal masks, and of hieroglyphs sculptured in bands across the confusion. They stood at intervals in the open woods, facing each other as they had faced each other for more than a thousand years, as if staring across the centuries into another era when men had also cleared and subjugated this forest.

Behind the first stone figure the broad ruins of a staircase, now overgrown with grass so that it had the appearance of a natural embankment, rose to a high terrace. On the other side I found a square plaza bounded by more embankments supporting ruined temples whose stone walls appeared in patches through the vegetation, the whole locked in by the towering wall of the forest. For more than a thousand years the people who had once danced in this plaza had been gone; but the birds, whose brilliant plumage had adorned the dancers' bodies, were still here, no different today than they had been then. The clearing was alive and ringing with them. Across the plaza, one or two at a time, came a steady procession of black toucans with yellow bibs and grotesque bills, flowing into a stripped ceiba which was like a forest in itself. With their long curved noses held horizontally before them they appeared half-reptilian, like flying lizards in that late-tadpole stage of evolution when they are about to become birds, having acquired bird-plumage but not yet having withdrawn their slim bodies into the compact form of the finished creation. They alternately flapped and rested on their wings, and as each landed the body broke, the long tail became a separate hinged appendage, the great yellow bill, stained with blue and crimson, pointed downward at right angles. Then they jumped softly from twig to twig, uttering gentle croaks that might have been made on a hollow wooden instrument. They were quiet and alert, like reptiles. The openwork of the ceiba was punctuated by their forms, moving with the usual abruptness of birds, but softly, as if afraid to awaken something. At the far side of the tree the procession moved out again toward the deep woods beyond, so that its population remained constant despite the unabated flow of new arrivals.

Another stream came into the same colony from another direction and was diverted downward into the low bush growing against the staircase. But these were toy toucans, the size of jays, in green, black, yellow, and red plumage, their bills distinctly serrated. While they had the same way of alternately winging and resting, the intermittent whir of their wings gave the impression of a little motor that was released and braked in turn. They jumped about the branches with more freedom than the big toucans, not afraid to express themselves in explosive whistles. The company moved together through the tree as though executing some complicated maneuver in which each individual had a distinct role. From the bottom corner, one after another, like children following each other into the water, they nose-dived into the dense bush below and were lost.

Obscure brown birds with sickle bills crept up and about tree-trunks, as unobtrusive as flakes of bark. Under a mass of foliage a violet, iridescent trogon sat silently, its head drawn forward, its heavy tail hanging straight. From moment to moment it would dart a few inches from its perch, hover under some leaves, and return; but moving so deftly that I noticed it only by accident. Under other bowers of leaves the glossy caciques, in twos and threes, hopped about and whistled liquidly.

This was what I had come for, to see the birds against this setting of the past. By now the sun had risen clear and shone over the enclosing wall of forest, the tree-trunks and twisted vines that rose from behind dense masses of foliage to meet other masses of foliage above. It shone with splendor over the pageantry that went on against this background. The hysterical shrieking of parrots tore through the silence of the trees. They hung from drooping boughs, chased each other screaming in and out through mazes of verdure, climbed about the branches with clumsy deliberation, took off for short labored flights, landed again, took off again. They circled out in pairs over the clearing, one just on top of the other, with a stiff vibration of their arched wings that seemed barely adequate to keep them aloft, their green bodies, scarlet foreheads, blue crowns, and yellow tails resplendent in the slanting sunlight. Or they landed on the topmost twigs of the low trees that grew from the temples, standing alert and silent for a moment, then screaming and pursuing each other out over the plaza again.

In the low bushes of the clearing a large colony of anis, their black plumage wet and sticky in appearance, sat about or teetered on the leaves with tails that dropped perpendicularly, like those celluloid birds with notches instead of feet that one sees perched on glass rings in florists' shops. Occasionally three or four would fly weakly across an open space, in single file, to join their companions in an adjacent bush, where they would allow their wings to droop in the sun and occasionally open their thick bills to voice a pair of harsh staccato whistles.

One of the big black toucans had found a berry which he rolled about in his open bill, out to the end and back again, like a ball in a slot. He jumped up to a limb above him, hopped along it till he came to another toucan, reached out with his bill, and let her take the berry from him.

In the white sky overhead swallows and swifts were milling, the swallows swarming about the treetops like hiving bees, the swifts remaining far up above the level of the forest. From time to time small groups of parrakeets came over. Oropendulas followed an unswerving line, flying with steady, uninterrupted beats of their broad wings, as if bent on such serious business that they could not be distracted for a moment (indeed, many of them carried nesting material). A large woodpecker came through the clearing in a series of long dips and brought up hard against the bole of a tree at the far side. He remained motionless for a moment, his head with scarlet crest and sharp ivory bill drawn back, then uttered two loud yelps, hitched himself up to a crotch, and disappeared on the other side. Turkey vultures, their silvery wings occasionally dipping in a slow stroke, swung in and out among the treetops, tilting as they turned. Then a heavy black hawk glided obliquely down into the clearing on set wings and swept up again to a branch in the upper stories of the forest beyond. He sat there massive and motionless, only pivoting his little head to glare about him.

Two parrots were suddenly fighting in the treetops. They grappled with each other, shrieking royally, and floated downward against the green of the forest, a single bundle of confusion from which loose feathers and down were shaken as from a mop.

This was what I had come for. These age-old occupants of a deserted city, each exclusively intent on the moment,

had seen the strange history of man performed here in miniature. What a story of ghosts they might tell if they could
speak of this clearing and the past!

When the men who built the temples and carved the
stone monuments first came into this valley—that must have
been some fifteen thousand years ago—they found these
same birds already in occupation. When they left the valley,
and that is well over a thousand years ago, these same birds
remained behind. And here they are today. These same
birds, these parrots and toucans, these caciques and these
hawks, have a past that goes far back of the history of man
in the New World, not only into the misty ages of ten thousand years ago, but into the outer darkness of a thousand
times ten thousand years; and then double or triple that.
You would have to go back over a hundred million years
for the first of all birds, as for the first mammal; but that
was not in the New World.

The story of the birds in this clearing of the forest, however, commences somewhat beyond a million years ago, before the polar ice-caps began their invasion of the middle
areas of the earth. A few of these birds—the parrots for one
—had already occupied the region, which by that time had
much the appearance it has today. What their ancestors had
been doing for a hundred million years before, since their
forefather, the archæopteryx, left his bones on the hills of
Bavaria, no one can say, but there must have been a good
deal of going to and fro in the earth. In any case, the earliest
of the birds in our present roster came from the south—
probably the Amazon valley—before the Ice Age, with a
host of others that were exterminated or driven back again
by the subsequent refrigeration of the climate. These sur-

vived and are still among us, having undergone some super-
ficial changes in color and size in the intervening years, but
remaining generically what they were when they first came.
The advance of the cold weather, which disposed of most
of their company, also brought in a fresh host of immigrants
from the north, of which few, however, remain in this particular region today (the red-winged blackbird of the vicinity is one of them).

The vireos, the blackbirds, and those others that came
here from the north at the beginning of the Ice Age knew
nothing of us men, as they had occasion to later; the most
imposing mammal they knew was the mastodon, but he
could not have appeared very dangerous to little flying birds.
For in those days our own forerunner, the ape-man of Java,
was running naked in the forests of another hemisphere.
But these birds knew nothing of him—or of his successors,
who would invent blow-guns and adorn their bodies with
bird-plumage. The valley belonged to them still, as much
as it belonged to anyone. Man had not yet entered the
Western Hemisphere.

In the time of Crô-Magnon Man—who may well be our
direct ancestor—the Ice Age came to an end, or at least another interglacial period set in (one would have to forecast
the future to tell which). As a result of the beneficent change
of climate a host of birds came flooding back into this region
from the south; while in the eastern hemisphere man suddenly burgeoned forth. Already only a few thousand years
from Ancient History when it began, we are still in the era
of that burgeoning, and the birds may still be flowing into
Central America from the south. Most of the species in this
clearing (the toucans, for example) are the products of this
current invasion.

But here, at the dawn of History, treating of this moment that began less than ten thousand years ago, one has to drop these attempts to conceive of inconceivable intervals of time. The explosion of man over the face of the earth, which is taking place this instant, is too stunningly sudden to be understood in terms of the whole. How it fits into the scheme of things, where it belongs in the slow transformation of life on this planet as exemplified by the birds, where it will land us—these are thoughts that may flash through our heads at the moment of the explosion; as a sailor whose ship is blown up under him might have time for two or three swift mental questions as he hurtled through the air. He could not really tell anything about what was happening, of course. Such questions must await the formal inquest of the proper officials after the event; at the moment there is only shock and bewilderment.

With all orthodox historians, then, one must pretend that man is completely apart from nature, that this strange explosive phenomenon, Human History, has nothing to do with the obscure and ponderous unfolding of Natural History in which the birds play their part.

Twenty or twenty-five thousand years ago (probably), while the birds and beasts of this valley were living in happy ignorance of the future, certain bands of Mongolians of whom we know nothing at all were wandering about the great expanses of Asia and coming closer to the one narrow bridge that, when the ice is frozen, connects the East with the West. A good guess has it that the first wanderers crossed the ice some twenty thousand years ago. But there was nothing casual or accidental about this invasion of what later came to be called the New World. Those first discoverers were at the outer edge of an expansion that had the impetus

of fate behind it. They were almost literally catapulted into
the New World by the centrifugal force which warm weather
and the invention of tools released. Man was suddenly increasing and spreading like an ink-blot over the landscape.

Meanwhile the birds, with slow accretions from the south,
were living their lives in this forest as they live it today, in
company with monkeys, jaguars, tapirs, sloths, and all the
lesser beasts that scuttle through the bush. Oropendulas, I
suppose, flew overhead with bits of nesting material in their
beaks, toucans croaked woodenly and hopped along the
branches with their peculiar soft movements, vultures
swept about the tops of the trees in search of death. And all
the time band after band of men was pushing south, entering new lands, giving way to the pressure of those who followed from the north. They flowed into valleys, through
gaps in the mountains, across plains; and in a few thousand
years they had flowed all over the face of two continents.
They came so far and so slowly (though it may seem rapid
in our perspective, events having an amazing way of dimin-
ishing so that a few thousand years of prehistoric time seem
less than our past calendar year), they came so far and so
slowly that they forgot where they had come from and
when; for they had no written language and kept no records. I dare say that when they were far enough advanced
to begin thinking of gods they attributed their existence,
along with that of the toucans and oropendulas, to a special
local Act of Creation, without considering whether there
might be other continents in the world with other men.

I have spent days traveling through this forest of Central
America, which stretches unbroken for hundreds of miles
to the north, a great wilderness of gigantic vegetation that
is once more inhabited only by the birds and beasts of ten

thousand years ago, with only the stone debris that lies scattered on its floor to tell of the cultural explosion that once took place here; and it is not difficult to picture the coming of the first men. They had smooth, flat, rounded faces, with fleshy Mongoloid features and an expression of primitive animal innocence in their dark, wide-open eyes. Their hair was long, straight, and glossy black; their naked bodies were a warm mahogany color; and they carried spears or, possibly, bows and arrows in their hands. Women came after them with infants at their breasts. The little bands of men moved quietly through the shadows of the woods, underneath the vegetation that opened before them and closed over their heads. Hummingbirds undoubtedly darted out to inspect them, monkeys leaped about in the branches, barking and chattering at them as they do today, jays made an hysterical commotion about their passage, warning all other birds and beasts with their screams and rendering futile the care of the hunters to be unnoticed. But some of the more reckless birds and monkeys met sudden death, of a kind they had not known before. Their bodies were stripped and eaten, their bones thrown to the dogs which, with the men, entered these woods for the first time. At night the hunters crouched about fire, making low grunting sounds. And then, perhaps, they vanished again, moving onward; though others followed and before long became a familiar sight in the forest, as much a part of the scenery as the animals who had inhabited it for hundreds of thousands of years before.

But now an extraordinary event took place practically simultaneously in the New World and the Old, showing that like causes produce like effects, or that human nature is the same the world over, or that Fate (or Kismet, or Providence, or whatever) knows no geographical boundaries: man took the second great step in his rise to dominion over the natural world. Having invented tools to begin with, he now laid the foundations of modern society by inventing agriculture. He laid the foundations in the very broadest sense, for once he had learned to plant and to harvest it was inevitable that he should build towns, create literature, paint pictures, carve stones, conceive religion, invent mathematics, develop forms of government, and divide himself into castes. It made possible a settled way of life, required careful observation of the seasons, the working out of a calendar and the conjuration of nature, brought people together into communities for which traditional laws and customs had to be established, the giving and taking in marriage arranged, punishment and reward dispensed. It brought justice, which meant Law; and leisure, which meant Freedom. In a word, it inaugurated History.

And with the inauguration of History began what might be termed a series of minor explosions within the greater explosion of man's expansion. Particular groups of men here and there in the world suddenly arose and developed at a prodigious rate, building cities, creating pantheons, broadening the spoken word into a written language capable of recording the complexities of their vision, learning to apply their tools to self-expression in sculpture and painting and architecture, and finally spreading out from their center with the force of a bombshell—till the original impulse was expended, the energy dissipated, and they sank back again toward their primitive beginnings or were overwhelmed by the explosion of another, younger culture at their borders.

It is certain that some three or four thousand years ago

the erstwhile nomads from Asia had settled down to growing corn in the highlands of Middle America, in the mountains above this valley, and were already learning to model
crude religious figurines in clay and propitiate the gods
who governed the seasons that governed the corn. At first,
as one conceives it, their methods were makeshift and they
prospered little; they knew almost nothing of the soil or
the seasons and so could not arrange their planting accordingly. The corn grew or it didn't grow. But these men,
like the birds, had keen powers of observation, and, unlike
the birds, they could draw remarkably just and complicated
conclusions from their observations, conclusions of which
they took advantage to mend their ways. They learned a
method of keeping permanent records on bits of grass, bark,
or wood, and before long they were calmly taking notes on
natural phenomena and putting them away for future reference. I imagine that if all nature could stand aghast, it did
so then. By the time Julius Cæsar had given our present
calendar to the Old World, these men had already worked
out an equally exact calendrical system, knew all that it was
necessary to know about the movements of the stars and
planets that ruled the wet and dry seasons, could predict
eclipses that would occur long after they were dead, and
boldly made their calculations in terms of hundreds of
thousands of years. It is profoundly shocking, when you
think of the slow march of ages that had gone before, and
no doubt there were Jeremiahs even in that day who cried
out woe. But history was in the making, the powder-train
had been fired.

Already the men who had been left behind in the Old
World had embarked on the series of historical cycles that
followed the invention of agriculture: in Egypt the Phar-

aohs ruled under the shadows of immense stone pyramids
that housed the remains of their ancestors, while in China a
feudal society was composing its classical literature. Some
three thousand years after the explosion had been set off in
Africa and in Europe, two or three thousand years after it
had been set off in the East, the fuse that had been smoldering in these isolated highlands reached its base in this
forest and touched off the first cultural explosion of the
New World.

The elements of a great historical culture in the western
hemisphere had been assembled and were ready for the unfolding. Some time in the early years of the Christian era,
when the ancient classical culture of Europe was already
crumbling, great cities arose and began to spread like a
rash over this forest till, in a century, they had reached beyond this valley to the mountains on the southern horizon.
Vast temples and palaces and pyramids were scattered for
hundreds of miles by that first explosion. Just as in the Old
World, these men organized themselves into city-states, conceived an epic literature and a society of gods to explain and
glorify their existence, created a special priesthood to deal
with Truth and the Mysteries of Being, and trained a class
of artisans to memorialize those Mysteries and that Truth
in the great stone monuments that today lie scattered and
broken on the jungle floor. Men suddenly seemed like gods,
nature gave way before them. The stars were charted, the
forest was reduced, the soil was made to give food, the birds
and beasts were killed, their fur and plumage taken from
them for the adornment of men's bodies. The chains with
which nature had held all life in bondage for thousands and
hundreds of thousands of centuries were suddenly broken

and man was free. He vanquished his enemies and, dancing before his stone altars, he sacrified them to the Mystery that had provided the means for his dominion.

The youthful belief in their own unconquerable strength, in their mission, in their very godhead, inspired the men who inhabited this forest to express on a stupendous scale the new selfhood of which they had become aware —not that old animal self, but the obscure soul that moved mightily in the heirs of the ape-man. Great blocks of stone were torn from the soil to receive the impressions of the new Truth, to carry the message and the inspiration to the generations of the future, to vanquish death. The secrets of the Mystery, carved into the everlasting rock, became all men's property for as long as stone endured and men could read. The body might die, but in these monuments the soul lived on.

The city in this clearing, raised during the days when Europe had sunk back into the Dark Ages, is not to be compared in scale with the cities farther north. It has neither the extent nor the gigantic architecture of the principal sites. But as an expression of the spirit of man it stands at the summit of this people's achievement, marking the Golden Age of their history. Lavishness and flamboyance, the pursuit of the spectacular, came later, when the spiritual impulse had atrophied into a desire for mere showiness, for pomp and splendor. In its stone faces and hieroglyphs this city records the youth and poetry of a great culture.

But youth and poetry, vision and ambition, are not for ever and ever. Nature works from within as well as without; death, with time on its side, is never quite vanquished. For men, once they have expressed the greatness that is in them, become tired, they lose their inspiration and doubt their divinity. Their work is done and still there is no rest except in death, in the final annihilation that they have for so long struggled to avert. In or about the large clearing adjacent to these temples stands a series of sixteen sculptured monoliths and one temple erected at five-year intervals over a period of sixty-five years, which is about the lifetime of a healthy man or a parrot. (Pericles lived sixty-five years, and gave his name to another Golden Age.) The first fifty years, as revealed by these stones, marked a phenomenally rapid rise in the mastery of the craft, from the archaic crudeness of the first shaft to the subtly refined and sophisticated intricacies of that figure of splendor seated in the jaws of the mythological monster. But already, before more than half that time had elapsed, the soaring ambition had met its first check. Having quarried ever larger stones for their monuments as their technique developed, the citizens of this valley outdid themselves in the twenty-fifth year by attempting to erect a shaft seven times as tall as a man and almost five times the height of the first of the series. For a dozen centuries, until some twenty years ago, that great stone statue stood in the ground at a crazy angle, a monument to their ambition and a monument to their first great failure. The next shaft that they raised, five years afterwards, was only half its size. Like the similarly naïve and youthful people who gave up the attempt to build a tower of unsurpassed height on the cathedral of Beauvais after it had fallen twice, they learned, for the first time, of their own limitations.

This speaks for one city only. Four hundred years before this era that marks the summit of their achievement, their Periclean Age, these people had raised their first great monuments in the forest to the north of here, beginning an

extraordinary efflorescence over the whole area that cul-
minated in this flash of glory. Likewise over the whole area,
the hundred years that followed showed a gradual falling
off, an exhaustion of the spirit that had inspired greatness,
now that greatness was accomplished. The flash of sheet-fire
dwindled to a flame. The Tower of Babel had been raised,
and still men were no nearer heaven. They had merely
found out for the first time that there is an insurmountable
barrier between the human and the divine.

*So the Lord scattered them abroad from thence upon the
face of all the earth: and they left off to build the city.*

Within a century of the failure to raise their greatest
stone, in those very years in which a barbarian chieftain in
the Old World was founding another Roman Empire and
inaugurating a new culture which was destined to spread,
this time, over the entire globe, the people who had labored
in this valley abandoned their city to time and retreated
into the wilderness once more. The impulse had spent itself. Their youth was over, their maturity had been achieved,
their long decay was before them. From east to west and
from north to south, over the whole extent of this forest,
they deserted the cities of their Golden Age. The trees
fastened their roots upon the sculptured stones and once
more the clearings were sealed. The birds and the beasts
again enjoyed shade where, for a time, there had been only
sunlight.

As for the men, the prophecy was fulfilled that their
language should be confounded "that they may not understand one another's speech." No longer held together by
the inspired vision and the invincible confidence of their
youth, distintegration set in among them. The new cities

that were raised in the north—lavish and pompous but lacking the spiritual purity of the earlier, no longer reaching to heaven—were soon at war with one another; the stone chisel of the artist became the battle-ax of the warrior; once peaceful communities were turned into armed camps and shed their blood. When, in another five centuries, the expansion of the new and still confident European culture reached the shores of the western hemisphere, it found these people far below the pinnacle of their one-time greatness and deep in the morass of their decline, a decadent race of dispirited men sinking slowly back to the primal level from which they had risen. The birds alone remained unchanged, once more confirmed in their immemorial possession of the forest.

Only dogs and Englishmen stay out in the midday sun. The dogs sleep, and the Englishmen, who are notoriously above all things natural or supernatural, never notice. But ordinary human beings and cattle search about for patches of shade and retreat under canopies of leaves while the sun makes its passage across the top of the sky. There is nothing gradual and insinuating about the sun in the tropics, as there is in the north. It pushes up over the horizon in one movement, without hesitation, and at the same moment the atmosphere is charged with radiant heat from the east. A veil of cloud above the horizon will help to soften that first impact, but even so a blind man could feel the sun rise. It is dramatic and profoundly satisfying. The heat strikes you, encompasses you, enfolds you, works into your bones, bakes your very brains, and thus puts you on your guard from the start. In the north the sun is halfway to the top of its course (which is never directly overhead, as it is here)

before you begin to feel uncomfortable, and by that time
you have already eaten too much breakfast and are dyspep-
tic, planned too much activity and are exhausted; the heat
seems just an intolerable interfering nuisance. But in the
tropics you don't underestimate the sun's hostility, you are
on your guard and prepared for it. You eat a light breakfast before dawn, and when the sun rises you can go out and
shake your fist at it. You know just what to expect. From six
to nine and from five to sunset the day is yours; otherwise
the sun is master and you plan accordingly.

By now this clearing was a welter of sunshine, the light
a blinding glory, and the heat beating down from above till
you might have poached an egg in your hat. It was no time
to be sitting out on the wall of a ruined temple whose roof,
which may once have sheltered a spot of coolness, lay in stone
fragments at your feet. The birds, having known this far-
too-benevolent sun for ages past counting, had retired and
only showed themselves occasionally about the edges of the
trees. Sometimes a handful of toucans would jump up into
the top of a tree out of nowhere, wing silently across a corner
of the clearing through open sunlight, and disappear into
nowhere again. Only the vultures, who love death and the
sun, grew more numerous as the other birds disappeared.
They came swinging and swaying on motionless wings, their
shadows running over the trees and temples without a
whisper, like fish shadows over the ocean floor. The clearing
was enchanted by light as the forest had been enchanted by
shadow. White and golden bits of jungle wall, incarnating
sunlight in the shape of butterflies, became detached and
went frolicking off about the edges of things to find another
place of attachment. From the depths of nowhere a voice
of pain took up a gentle, persistent cooing and forgot to

leave off. The old city seemed stunned with the sheer daze of glory. I got up for a moment, allowing the sun to strike the stone I had so far kept reasonably cool, and then I could not sit down again. In any case, I was neither dog nor Englishman, so I swam away through the dazzle, my feet plowing up the grass and stumbling over fallen stones.

The tall stone shafts, standing at irregular intervals in an area about the size of a polo-field, were shaded by trees just thick enough to form an imperfect canopy overhead through which the sunlight streaked and fell in patches to the ground. One might think from the casual, competent, and confident way in which archæologists and wandering amateurs write of these stones that everything about them is known. As a matter of fact, most of what one sees on the subject is just ignorance dressed up in surmise. It's a game of surmises, really, in which each player puts his particular stack of guesses on the table and tries to win credit for them. One stack is played against another, and the player with the best hand sometimes wins. But the best hand still consists only of a pack of surmises. Nothing is known *for-a-fact*. The old Mayas who inhabited the forests of Guatemala and southern Mexico may have come from the north, from the south, from the east, from the west, or they may have arisen right here by the spontaneous generation of decaying vegetation. They may have been blown in on clouds by the trade-winds and deposited like rain. The seas may have divided, or a roc may have ferried them over from Arabia, for all the certainty there is in the matter. But sobriety is one of the credits of the game, and that is why most of the best players will tell you that the American Indians are a Mongoloid stock that crossed over into this hemisphere from Asia by way of the Bering Straits. But, though they may state

it for a fact (that is part of the game), it is not actually known
for a fact.

Some also state for a fact that these stones are portraits
of contemporary Mayan potentates, and I am perfectly content that it should be so. But, for all the evidence they have,
these are still just faces in the jungle. Not having a professional reputation at stake, I rather cherish the mystery
which, after a century of intensive research, remains as
virginal as in the days when the first startled European con-
querors, cutting their way through this forest, were confronted by impassive stone faces in their path. *Alles Ver-
gängliche ist nur ein Gleichnis.*

Potentates they may have been, and gods they may have
been, for at a certain level the two become indistinguish-
able. The naked face is manifestly the face of the Indian,
luxuriously torpid with the weight of the centuries, the
lips parted voluptuously as if in dream. His sleep, however,
is not the sleep of death but a sleep that breathes and glows
with latent vitality. He is ready to wake up and start into
life again at any moment, and some day, when the affairs
of the world are wound up and finality is achieved, you feel
quite sure he will. These stones, which have preserved a
life in death, are a sermon on immortality.

Once, recently, a traveler came here and remained just
long enough to deliver his judgment on these faces that had
confronted the jungle undisturbed through a dozen centuries. He found them not beautiful, and took to task those
who thought otherwise. Mystical nonsense, he called it,
and more to that effect. Diminished as I was by their living
grandeur, I could not find within me the presumption to
defend them. But those poor Mayas! Ten centuries they
labored to leave their mark in the wild forest that has long

since obliterated all else, breaking their backs beneath the burden of a vision that mastered them as it had mastered the Prophets. . . . Was it merely that a twentieth-century tourist might exclaim: "Nothing to it," and turn away to catch the next train back?

But the final judgment is not yet. Long after the impetuous tourist and I have both passed into outer darkness and been forgotten, these living images will stand, and the birds will fly overhead into a future that no one can foretell.

8593